STRESSED,
Unstressed

STRESSED, Unstressed

classic poems to ease the mind

edited by
Jonathan Bate
Paula Byrne
Sophie Ratcliffe
and
Andrew Schuman

with an afterword by
Mark Williams

WILLIAM
COLLINS

William Collins
An imprint of HarperCollins Publishers
1 London Bridge Street
London SE1 9GF
www.WilliamCollinsBooks.com

First published in Great Britain by William Collins in 2016

1 3 5 7 9 8 6 4 2

A catalogue record for this book is
available from the British Library.

ISBN 978-0-00-816450-8

Printed and bound in Great Britain by
Clays Ltd, St Ives plc

MIX
Paper from
responsible sources
FSC™ C007454

contents

These poems were selected by Jonathan Bate, Paula Byrne, Sophie Ratcliffe and Andrew Schuman, who all contributed to the section introductions. Many of the poems have been tried and tested in healthcare settings or at stressful times, past and present. Proceeds from sales of the anthology will be donated to ReLit, the campaign of the Bibliotherapy Foundation (a charitable enterprise) to alleviate stress and other mental health conditions through mindful reading. For more information about the work of the Foundation, please visit www.relit.org.uk.

We would love to hear about the ways in which this anthology, and poetry in general, has helped you. Please add your comments on our website www.relit.org.uk/stressed.

introduction

'Words are, of course, the most powerful
drug used by mankind'
Rudyard Kipling

There are many ways of dealing with stress: a walk in the park, a cup of tea and a chat with a friend, a long hot bath, or that form of practised meditation which has become known as 'mindfulness'. In this little book, we would like to share another remedy, in fact one of the oldest remedies of all: the reading of poetry.

True poetry, claimed William Wordsworth, is either 'the spontaneous overflow of powerful feelings' or 'emotion recollected in tranquillity'. The idea for this anthology came from the recollection of the powerful feelings stirred by some life-changing moments. There was a thirteen-year-old girl who lost her father and found comfort in a four-hundred-year-old poem by John Donne. There was the sense of utter desolation on being told by a compassionate consultant that a five-year-old daughter in intensive care could not be guaranteed to survive the night: hope came from a remembered poem that gave a glimpse of how others have endured their own desolation and come out the other side. Then there was the need to fill the mind with beautiful words and rich thoughts while waiting through many hours of surgery as that same child received a life-saving transplant.

There was also the experience of stress so intense that it manifested itself as physical pain in the hands and feet that was as real as that of an organic condition: yet the pain evaporated when a creative general practitioner prescribed not a drug but a book that provided exercises for managing stress. This inspired the thought: if words can do the work of drugs, what is to lose by putting them in our mental health first aid kit?

There is nothing to lose and everything to gain. The great eighteenth-century reader and writer Dr Samuel Johnson said that the only purpose of literature was to enable the reader better to enjoy life or better to endure it. We offer some poems that provide pure (even nonsensical) enjoyment, but most of our selections are intended to help you endure some of your stressful moments and painful experiences. Among the themes to which poets have returned again and again over the centuries are love and death and memory – remembrance of childhood, of happy days and beautiful places, of loved ones we have lost, or of feeling at peace and at one with the natural world. We have harvested an array of classic poems on such themes in the hope that they will speak to you when you are processing your worries or when you simply want to fill your mind with different, more positive thoughts.

As 'Poems on the Underground' have for many years been momentary mental oases for stressed-out London commuters, so this volume of enduring classics and forgotten gems is intended for the waiting room, the sickbed, the sleepless night, the day when everything seems to be going wrong, the moment of respite. Keep it by your bed or stash it in your bag.

For centuries, people have turned to poetry in dark times. The philosopher John Stuart Mill told in his *Autobiography* of how reading the poetry of William Wordsworth cured him from depression. Queen Victoria said that Poet Laureate Alfred Tennyson's *In Memoriam*, a sequence of elegies working through his grief at the loss of his beloved friend Arthur Hallam, was the only means other than the Bible through which she coped with the death of Prince Albert. Poetry anthologies, most notably the *Golden Treasury* of Francis Turner Palgrave, were life-savers as much for soldiers resting behind the lines on the Western Front during the First World War as for young Victorian women suffering the kind of nervous complaints that now manifest themselves in eating disorders, exhaustion and worse. Tennyson said that Palgrave's book was 'able to sweeten solitude itself with the best society – with the companionship of the wise and the good, with the beauty which the eye cannot see, and the music heard only in silence'. And that is what we hope might be achieved in some small measure by our own selection, to which a range of readers and poetry-minded medical practitioners have contributed.

If poetry has the power that we – and so many others – claim for it, where does that power come from? Poems are language in concentrated form. They make you feel and make you think. They take you out of yourself, transport you to other worlds, away from your present troubles. Because they use words with beauty and care, they demand to be read with attention and without rush. The words must be savoured, because they are the linguistic equivalent of the best food and wine. Most of the time, we fill our minds with words that are the equivalent of fast food. Poetry is slow mind food, real nutrition for the soul. Attentive reading slows the breath and empties the mind of other cares. Especially if read aloud, and slowly, the rhythms of a good poem may be inherently calming and therapeutic, regardless of the subject matter. At the same time, the subject matter of poetry – memory, love, the restorative power of nature, confrontation with sorrow and death – often serves for attentive readers as a mirror of their own feelings, a welcome discovery that we are not alone in our own dark or anxious state.

The chime of rhyme, the reassurance of repetition, the sense of balance in the pattern of a stanza or the fourteen lines of a sonnet: all of these are formal devices which poets use to bring order to the chaos of experience and a sense of musical harmony, of *resolution*. But the basis of poetry is the alternating rhythm of stressed and unstressed syllables that replicates the beating of the human heart.

> **Tiger tiger, burning bright**
> **In the forests of the night**

Stressed, unstressed, stressed, unstressed: we hope you will discover that this poetic pattern, in its limitless variety, leads you to a calmer mental and physical state.

Next time you are feeling stressed or anxious, worried or sleepless, panicky or unable to cope, we invite you to choose a short poem at random from this book and perform a little exercise in what might be called 'word cure' or, to use the technical term, 'bibliotherapy'.

Make yourself comfortable. Try to clear your head of all your worries. Breathe slowly and regularly. Listen to your own breathing as you breathe in and out: already you will feel slightly calmer. Now read slowly through your chosen poem, maybe in your head, ideally aloud, perhaps both. Then immerse yourself in its words. Poems are often made by building a series of interconnected images. Look through your chosen poem again, finding the images. Try to recreate each successive image in your head, one at a time. Now, having focused on the component parts, imagine the whole as a little world of its own that you can hold in your mind's eye. You will perhaps find yourself recreating a calming landscape or a movement from troubled questioning to a sense of resolution.

By entering into the harmonized world of the poem, you have momentarily escaped your own world of stress and worry. Now you can slowly return to yourself, in the knowledge that you can find an oasis of calm, of beauty, and of belonging in the world. Now step back and ask yourself if you feel different from how you did before.

If the exercise has had any effect on you, then you are someone for whom this book is meant. Read on. You will find a few thoughts and suggestions at the beginning of each section. Our idea, as you work through the anthology, is that you begin by simply absorbing yourself in the moment, in the words of the poem, and that this will bring you mental relief and release. Then in later sections you will find poems that address experiences such as bereavement, heartbreak and depression, and we hope that you will take comfort in recognizing your own experiences in the lives of others.

And don't worry if the language or the thought patterns of some of these poems – especially the ones written in more distant centuries – seems difficult. You don't have to work it all out or turn to a dictionary; you can still enjoy the rhythms and the verbal inventiveness. Especially if you read aloud. Some readers take a special pleasure in learning poems by heart – the rhythmic beat and the brevity of the lines make that easier than other forms of rote learning. Who can forget, once they have read them – as you just have – the opening two lines of William Blake's 'Tiger'? And a poem committed to memory can often serve as a kind of mantra in times of stress: just by reciting it, we refocus ourselves.

In reading this anthology, you will take command of more than a hundred of the best poems ever written. You will enter the minds, and form a connection with, some extraordinarily creative men and women. Even those who are long dead live on through their words. You will go beyond your own circumstances, glimpse other lives and other levels of feeling. You will develop a sense of wonder in the beauty and strangeness of the world, together with deep admiration for the powers of human endurance and verbal expression. Above all, you will enter into a shared experience with the poets themselves and the countless others who have read and remembered and loved their poems. You will become part of an immortal community.

Jonathan Bate

1.

stopping

Remember the old road safety advice? Stop, look, listen. Here are some poems that may help us to de-stress by doing just that. Stopping by woods on a walk; a train stopped in a station; stopping to taste a plum, to look at a wheelbarrow, to marvel at a tree or even to observe a spider.

Our bodies operate, for the most part, below the radar – under the control of the so-called autonomic nervous system. The conscious part of the brain and nervous system lets us know when (and exactly how) to move our hand in order, say, to turn the pages of this book. But the unconscious workings of the nervous system are far more covert. We use two different groups of nerve fibres to manage our unconscious processes: 'parasympathetic' nerves deal with our everyday bodily functions – things like urination and digestion. By contrast, the 'sympathetic' nerves, activated by a chemical called adrenalin, fire up when we are under pressure and stress. This is the so-called 'fight or flight' response. Sometimes our 'sympathetic' nerve fibres go into overdrive, and we produce too much adrenalin for our own good. We end up on feeling on high alert – on our way to a big meeting or to a job interview, or, in some cases, just at the thought of leaving the house in the morning. We're left with a racing heart, sweaty palms and shaking limbs (symptoms that are useful only when, for example, you're being chased by a lion). It's a vicious cycle. The body makes us feel anxious, and the anxiety makes the physical symptoms worse. Doctors sometimes prescribe drugs, called beta-blockers, that stop the adrenalin from producing these symptoms.

Engaging with the initial feel of a poem on the page – its tempo, rhythm and cadences (its musicality) – then with the images it creates in the mind, and finally with its sense and possible meanings can help restore the balance of the para-sympathetic and sympathetic fibres. The 'fight or flight' adrenalin rush of the sympathetic nervous system starts to melt away, and gradually, as our breathing slows and as our racing pulse subsides, the less stressed and anxious we feel. A sense of calm can follow. Repetition (in a poem, and with repeated readings of a poem) brings with it a sense of familiarity, and is a step towards learning it off by heart. With a little time and effort, a poem can exist *in its entirety* in the brain of the reader, to be recalled at whatever moment it's most needed. A beta-blocker for the soul.

Stopping by Woods on a Snowy Evening

Whose woods these are I think I know.
His house is in the village though;
He will not see me stopping here
To watch his woods fill up with snow.

My little horse must think it queer
To stop without a farmhouse near
Between the woods and frozen lake
The darkest evening of the year.

He gives his harness bells a shake
To ask if there is some mistake.
The only other sound's the sweep
Of easy wind and downy flake.

The woods are lovely, dark and deep,
But I have promises to keep,
And miles to go before I sleep,
And miles to go before I sleep.

Robert Frost

Adlestrop

Yes. I remember Adlestrop –
The name, because one afternoon
Of heat the express-train drew up there
Unwontedly. It was late June.

The steam hissed. Someone cleared his throat.
No one left and no one came
On the bare platform. What I saw
Was Adlestrop – only the name

And willows, willow-herb, and grass,
And meadowsweet, and haycocks dry,
No whit less still and lonely fair
Than the high cloudlets in the sky.

And for that minute a blackbird sang
Close by, and round him, mistier,
Farther and farther, all the birds
Of Oxfordshire and Gloucestershire.

Edward Thomas

Five Senses

Now my five senses
gather into a meaning
all acts, all presences;
and as a lily gathers
the elements together,
in me this dark and shining,
that stillness and that moving,
these shapes that spring from nothing,
become a rhythm that dances,
a pure design.

While I'm in my five senses
they send me spinning
all sounds and silences,
all shape and colour
as thread for that weaver,
whose web within me growing
follows beyond my knowing
some pattern sprung from nothing –
a rhythm that dances
and is not mine.

Judith Wright

The Small Window

In Wales there are jewels
To gather, but with the eye
Only. A hill lights up
Suddenly; a field trembles
With colour and goes out
In its turn; in one day
You can witness the extent
Of the spectrum and grow rich
With looking. Have a care;
This wealth is for the few
And chosen. Those who crowd
A small window dirty it
With their breathing, though sublime
And inexhaustible the view.

R. S. Thomas

Red Wheelbarrow

so much depends
upon

a red wheel
barrow

glazed with rain
water

beside the white
chickens.

William Carlos Williams

From **Auguries of Innocence**

To see a world in a grain of sand
And a heaven in a wild flower,
Hold infinity in the palm of your hand,
And eternity in an hour.

William Blake

Green

The dawn was apple-green,
The sky was green wine held up in the sun,
The moon was a golden petal between.

She opened her eyes, and green
They shone, clear like flowers undone
For the first time, now for the first time seen.

D. H. Lawrence

Trees

Elm trees
and the leaf the boy in me hated
long ago –
rough and sandy.

Poplars
and their leaves,
tender, smooth to the fingers,
and a secret in their smell
I have forgotten.

Oaks
and forest glades,
heart aching with wonder, fear:
their bitter mast.

Willows
and the scented beetle
we put in our handkerchiefs;
and the roots of one
that spread into a river:
nakedness, water and joy.

Hawthorn,
white and odorous with blossom,
framing the quiet fields,
and swaying flowers and grasses,
and the hum of bees.

Oh, these are the things that are with me now,
in the town;
and I am grateful
for this minute of my manhood.

F. S. Flint

A Noiseless Patient Spider

A noiseless patient spider,
I marked where on a promontory it stood isolated,
Marked how to explore the vacant vast surrounding,
It launched forth filament, filament, filament, out of
    itself,
Ever unreeling them, ever tirelessly speeding them.

And you O my soul where you stand,
Surrounded, detached, in measureless oceans of space,
Ceaselessly musing, venturing, throwing, seeking the
    spheres to connect them,
Till the bridge you will need be formed, till the ductile
    anchor hold,
Till the gossamer thread you fling catch somewhere, O
    my soul.

Walt Whitman

This Is Just To Say

I have eaten
the plums
that were in
the icebox

and which
you were probably
saving
for breakfast

Forgive me
they were delicious
so sweet
and so cold

William Carlos Williams

Leisure

What is this life if, full of care,
We have no time to stand and stare? –

No time to stand beneath the boughs,
And stare as long as sheep and cows:

No time to see, when woods we pass,
Where squirrels hide their nuts in grass:

No time to see, in broad daylight,
Streams full of stars, like skies at night:

No time to turn at Beauty's glance,
And watch her feet, how they can dance:

No time to wait till her mouth can
Enrich that smile her eyes began?

A poor life this if, full of care,
We have no time to stand and stare.

W. H. Davies

2.

composing

'Compose yourself': that is what we sometimes say to ourselves when we are stressed or flustered. Calm down, take things moment by moment, organize your thoughts. The word 'compose' comes from the Latin meaning 'putting things together'. That is to say, creating order. Poets, like those who write music, are composers. They take emotions and ideas and words and put them into harmonious, melodious order. There is no better example of this process than the special form of poetry known as the sonnet. It is a form that has certain rules – though great poets always know how to bend the rules. You need fourteen lines, a regular five-beat rhythm, a pattern of rhymes and perhaps a twist in the tale. The name is derived from the Italian word 'sonetto', a little song. When we read a great sonnet, our appreciation of the poet's ordering of thoughts – about love or beauty or sorrow or time or almost anything – can help us to compose ourselves.

You can take this to a deeper level. As science writer Philip Ball argues, 'our brains are attuned to finding regularities in the world' – and they respond to patterns 'aesthetically'. Try looking at one of the sonnets that follow as if it were a kind of visual or musical pattern. Maybe take a pencil and circle the alternating rhymes. Or speak it out loud and see if you can hear a regularity of rhythm. When we find a pattern – whether it is in the regular coil of a snail's shell, the 'fearful symmetry' of Blake's tiger, or the movements of a poem – our brain gets a kind of rush, which Ball calls 'the pleasure and satisfaction of seeing universal harmonies'.

Paradoxically, a poem can give us just this kind of brain-rush in the very same moment that it encourages us to slow down our thought processes or to be still and observe the world around us. Wordsworth's 'Upon Westminster Bridge' is especially soothing and reflective. In July 1802 he and his sister Dorothy were crossing the bridge in a coach on the way to France early on a cloudless summer morning, when the city was still sleeping and bathed in golden light: 'Ne'er saw I, never felt, a calm so deep'. It invites the reader to read the sonnet slowly, meditatively, pausing with each reflection: 'The beauty of the morning: silent, bare, / Ships, towers, domes, theatres, and temples lie'.

Similarly, R. S. Thomas, in his 'Bright Field', which keeps to the fourteen lines but relaxes the rules for stressed syllables and rhyme, urges us to remember that life should not be rushed. Hurrying is an illusory quest for 'a receding future', which is an unhealthy as 'hankering after / an imagined past'. We must make time for 'turning aside'.

Upon Westminster Bridge

Earth has not anything to show more fair:
Dull would he be of soul who could pass by
A sight so touching in its majesty:
This City now doth, like a garment, wear
The beauty of the morning: silent, bare,
Ships, towers, domes, theatres, and temples lie
Open unto the fields, and to the sky;
All bright and glittering in the smokeless air.
Never did sun more beautifully steep
In his first splendour, valley, rock, or hill;
Ne'er saw I, never felt, a calm so deep!
The river glideth at his own sweet will:
Dear God! the very houses seem asleep;
And all that mighty heart is lying still!

William Wordsworth

Sonnet 116

Let me not to the marriage of true minds
Admit impediments. Love is not love
Which alters when it alteration finds,
Or bends with the remover to remove:
O no; it is an ever-fixèd mark,
That looks on tempests, and is never shaken;
It is the star to every wandering bark,
Whose worth's unknown, although his height be taken.
Love's not Time's fool, though rosy lips and cheeks
Within his bending sickle's compass come;
Love alters not with his brief hours and weeks,
But bears it out even to the edge of doom.
   If this be error and upon me proved,
   I never writ, nor no man ever loved.

William Shakespeare

Bright Star

Bright star, would I were steadfast as thou art –
Not in lone splendour hung aloft the night
And watching, with eternal lids apart,
Like nature's patient, sleepless Eremite,
The moving waters at their priest-like task
Of pure ablution round earth's human shores,
Or gazing on the new soft-fallen mask
Of snow upon the mountains and the moors –
No – yet still steadfast, still unchangeable,
Pillowed upon my fair love's ripening breast,
To feel for ever its soft fall and swell,
Awake for ever in a sweet unrest,
Still, still to hear her tender-taken breath,
And so live ever – or else swoon to death.

John Keats

Open Winter

Where slanting banks are always with the sun
The daisy is in blossom even now;
And where warm patches by the hedges run
The cottager when coming home from plough
Brings home a cowslip root in flower to set.
Thus ere the Christmas goes the spring is met
Setting up little tents about the fields
In sheltered spots. – Primroses when they get
Behind the wood's old roots, where ivy shields
Their crimpled, curdled leaves, will shine and hide.
Cart ruts and horses' footings scarcely yield
A slur for boys, just crizzled and that's all.
Frost shoots his needles by the small dyke side,
And snow in scarce a feather's seen to fall.

John Clare

Sonnets from the Portuguese 22

When our two souls stand up erect and strong,
Face to face, silent, drawing nigh and nigher,
Until the lengthening wings break into fire
At either curvèd point, – what bitter wrong
Can the earth do to us, that we should not long
Be here contented? Think. In mounting higher,
The angels would press on us, and aspire
To drop some golden orb of perfect song
Into our deep, dear silence. Let us stay
Rather on earth, Belovèd, – where the unfit
Contrarious moods of men recoil away
And isolate pure spirits, and permit
A place to stand and love in for a day,
With darkness and the death-hour rounding it.

Elizabeth Barrett Browning

Methought I saw my late espousèd saint

Methought I saw my late espousèd saint
   Brought to me, like Alcestis, from the grave,
   Whom Jove's great son to her glad husband gave,
   Rescued from death by force, though pale and faint.
Mine, as whom washed from spot of child-bed taint
   Purification in the old Law did save,
   And such as yet once more I trust to have
   Full sight of her in Heaven without restraint,
Came vested all in white, pure as her mind;
   Her face was veiled, yet to my fancied sight
   Love, sweetness, goodness, in her person shined
So clear as in no face with more delight.
   But Oh! as to embrace me she inclined,
   I waked, she fled, and day brought back my night.

John Milton
Remembering his wife, written when blind

Sonnet 18

Shall I compare thee to a summer's day?
Thou art more lovely and more temperate:
Rough winds do shake the darling buds of May,
And summer's lease hath all too short a date:
Sometime too hot the eye of heaven shines,
And often is his gold complexion dimmed,
And every fair from fair sometime declines,
By chance, or nature's changing course untrimmed:
But thy eternal summer shall not fade,
Nor lose possession of that fair thou ow'st,
Nor shall death brag thou wander'st in his shade,
When in eternal lines to time thou grow'st,
   So long as men can breathe, or eyes can see,
   So long lives this, and this gives life to thee.

William Shakespeare

One day I wrote her name upon the strand

One day I wrote her name upon the strand,
But came the waves and washèd it away:
Again I wrote it with a second hand,
But came the tide, and made my pains his prey.
'Vain man,' said she, 'that dost in vain assay,
A mortal thing so to immortalize;
For I myself shall like to this decay,
And eke my name be wipèd out likewise.'
'Not so,' (quod I) 'let baser things devise
To die in dust, but you shall live by fame:
My verse your virtues rare shall eternize,
And in the heavens write your glorious name:
Where whenas death shall all the world subdue,
Our love shall live, and later life renew.'

Edmund Spenser

When I have fears

When I have fears that I may cease to be
   Before my pen has gleaned my teeming brain,
Before high-pilèd books, in charactery,
   Hold like rich garners the full ripened grain;
When I behold, upon the night's starred face,
   Huge cloudy symbols of a high romance,
And think that I may never live to trace
   Their shadows with the magic hand of chance;
And when I feel, fair creature of an hour,
   That I shall never look upon thee more,
Never have relish in the faery power
   Of unreflecting love – then on the shore
Of the wide world I stand alone, and think
   Till love and fame to nothingness do sink.

John Keats

The Bright Field

I have seen the sun break through
to illuminate a small field
for a while, and gone my way
and forgotten it. But that was the
pearl of great price, the one field that had
treasure in it. I realise now
that I must give all that I have
to possess it. Life is not hurrying
on to a receding future, nor hankering after
an imagined past. It is the turning
aside like Moses to the miracle
of the lit bush, to a brightness
that seemed as transitory as your youth
once, but is the eternity that awaits you.

R. S. Thomas

3.

meditating

Many people have great success in dealing with stress by means of meditation or 'mindfulness'. This is an ancient practice, with its origins in Buddhist and other Eastern traditions. But meditation in the abstract can be difficult. It doesn't work for everybody. Immersion in a short contemplative poem works well as a form of meditation because the words and the images they create can help you to focus, to clear your mind of every other thought. This section begins with some very short poems, glimpses of grace captured in an instant. They are translated or adapted from ancient Chinese and Japanese traditions, the poetry of the Tang dynasty and the miniaturist art of the haiku. In the East, not least under Buddhist influence, the meditative moment has long been the bedrock of poetry. The Tang dynasty poets were typically court officials or civil servants who wrote poetry as a form of relaxation and inner calming when they retreated from the hectic, competitive world of work into the peace of the countryside. Each short piece offers a single image or brief chain of images. Empty your mind of other thoughts by absorbing yourself in the words, bringing alive the images in your imagination, taking yourself into the moment shared by the poet.

The world of nature is at the heart of much poetry written in English too. Relieve your stress by transporting yourself to some natural objects, places and moods of calm through the poems in this section: a beautiful lake remembered from a busy city street; a cherry tree in blossom; a quiet evening as birds return to their nests. Find your own oasis. Try noting down some images that conjure it up: you will have taken your own first step towards the writing of poetry.

Seven Ancient Japanese Haiku

I come weary,
In search of an inn –
Ah! these wisteria flowers!

An ancient pond!
With a sound from the water
Of the frog as it plunges in.

On a withered branch
A crow is sitting
This autumn eve.

The cry of the cicada
Gives us no sign
That presently it will die.

Thought I, the fallen flowers
Are returning to their branch;
But lo! they were butterflies.

Drinking tea alone:
every day the butterfly
stops by.

The world of dew
Is a world of dew,
And yet, and yet.

Translated by W. G. Aston
The first four are by Basho,
the fifth by Arakida Moritake
and the last two by Kobayashi Issa

from *Narrow Road to the Deep North*

It is with awe
That I beheld
Fresh leaves, green leaves,
Bright in the sun.

The chestnut by the eaves
In magnificent bloom
Passes unnoticed
By men of the world.

I felt quite at home,
As if it were mine,
Sleeping lazily
In this house of fresh air.

In the utter silence
Of a temple,
A cicada's voice alone
Penetrates the rocks.

Cranes hop around
On the watery beach of Shiogoshi
Dabbling their long legs
In the cool tide of the sea.

I hope to have gathered
To repay your kindness
The willow leaves
Scattered in the garden.

As firmly cemented clam shells
Fall apart in autumn,
So I must take to the road again,
Farewell, my friends.

Basho, translated by Nobuyuki Yuasa

Tang Variations

1. Deer Enclosure

Empty mountain. Seeing nobody.
Only hearing the sound of voices.
Reflection: sunlight enters the deep forest
And shines again on green moss.

2. House in the Bamboo Grove

Sitting alone deep in a remote thicket
I pluck my lute and sing.
In this dark unknown forest
The bright moon shines on me.

3. Goodbye

We go to the mountain for our farewell
At sunset I close the door in the brushwood fence
Next year the spring grass will be green
And you, prince among friends, will return or not return.

4. One Heart

Red beans grow in the south country
In the warm weather there will be many branches
I want you to be here to pluck them with me
That is the thing I yearn for: it will cure my heart.

5. A Farewell

If you return to the mountains and the valleys
You must find beauty in the heights and the depths:
Don't follow the example of the man
Who never travels beyond the peach garden where we
   play.

6. Snowy Peak

The north peak of Zhong Nan is beautiful
The snow piled up to the floating clouds
The sky is a blue clearing above the treetops
And the city below chills with the sunset.

7. Mooring at Night on Jiande River

Steering his boat to its berth beside the mist-smoke river
The failing light brings new sadness to the traveller
A wilderness of sky dwarfing the trees
But the clear river brings him close to the moon.

8. Spring Morning

Spring sleep does not feel the dawn
It hears the birds singing everywhere.
The night came with the sound of wind and rain
And I wonder how many blossoms fell.

9. Quiet Night Thinking

Bright moonlight on my bed
Like frost on hardened ground.
I raise my head and look at that bright moon
I bow my head and think of my old home.

10. Love's Bitterness

A beautiful woman rolls up a blind made of pearl
In deep stillness she sits with a little frown
Her eyebrow is like a moth
All I can see are the wet traces of her tears:
I do not know for whom she is crying,
Regret or hatred in her heart.

11. Climbing White Stork Tower

The white sun sets behind the mountain
The Yellow River flows into the sea
If you want to see a thousand miles
Then go up another floor, always up.

Eleven improvisations on ancient Chinese poems
by Wang Wei, Pei Di, Zu Young, Meng Haoran,
Li Bai, Wang Zhihuan

The Lake Isle of Innisfree

I will arise and go now, and go to Innisfree,
And a small cabin build there, of clay and wattles made;
Nine bean-rows will I have there, a hive for the
    honey-bee,
And live alone in the bee-loud glade.

And I shall have some peace there, for peace comes
    dropping slow,
Dropping from the veils of the morning to where the
    cricket sings;
There midnight's all a glimmer, and noon a purple glow,
And evening full of the linnet's wings.

I will arise and go now, for always night and day
I hear lake water lapping with low sounds by the shore;
While I stand on the roadway, or on the pavements grey,
I hear it in the deep heart's core.

W. B. Yeats

Birds at Evening

I love to hear the autumn crows go by
And see the starnels darken down the sky;
The bleaching stack the bustling sparrow leaves,
And plops with merry note beneath the eaves.
The odd and lated pigeon bounces by,
As if a wary watching hawk was nigh,
While far and fearing nothing, high and slow,
The stranger birds to distant places go;
While short of flight the evening robin comes
To watch the maiden sweeping out the crumbs,
Nor fears the idle shout of passing boy,
But pecks about the door, and sings for joy;
Then in the hovel where the cows are fed
Finds till the morning comes a pleasant bed.

John Clare

Loveliest of trees, from *A Shropshire Lad*

Loveliest of trees, the cherry now
Is hung with bloom along the bough,
And stands about the woodland ride
Wearing white for Eastertide.

Now, of my threescore years and ten,
Twenty will not come again,
And take from seventy springs a score,
It only leaves me fifty more.

And since to look at things in bloom
Fifty springs are little room,
About the woodlands I will go
To see the cherry hung with snow.

A. E. Housman

To the Fox Fern

Haunter of woods, lone wilds and solitudes
Where none but feet of birds and things as wild
Doth print a foot track near, where summer's light
Buried in boughs forgets its glare and round thy crimpèd
    leaves
Faints in a quiet dimness fit for musings
And melancholy moods, with here and there
A golden thread of sunshine stealing through
The evening shadowy leaves that seem to creep
Like leisure in the shade.

John Clare

April Rise

If ever I saw blessing in the air
I see it now in this still early day
Where lemon-green the vaporous morning drips
Wet sunlight on the powder of my eye.

Blown bubble-film of blue, the sky wraps round
Weeds of warm light whose every root and rod
Splutters with soapy green, and all the world
Sweats with the bead of summer in its bud.

If ever I heard blessing it is there
Where birds in trees that shoals and shadows are
Splash with their hidden wings and drops of sound
Break on my ears their crests of throbbing air.

Pure in the haze the emerald sun dilates,
The lips of sparrows milk the mossy stones,
While white as water by the lake a girl
Swims her green hand among the gathered swans.

Now, as the almond burns its smoking wick,
Dropping small flames to light the candled grass;
Now, as my low blood scales its second chance,
If ever world were blessed, now it is.

Laurie Lee

To Autumn

Season of mists and mellow fruitfulness,
Close bosom-friend of the maturing sun;
Conspiring with him how to load and bless
With fruit the vines that round the thatch-eves run;
To bend with apples the mossed cottage-trees,
And fill all fruit with ripeness to the core;
To swell the gourd, and plump the hazel shells
With a sweet kernel; to set budding more,
And still more, later flowers for the bees,
Until they think warm days will never cease,
For Summer has o'er-brimmed their clammy cells.

Who hath not seen thee oft amid thy store?
Sometimes whoever seeks abroad may find
Thee sitting careless on a granary floor,
Thy hair soft-lifted by the winnowing wind;
Or on a half-reaped furrow sound asleep,
Drowsed with the fume of poppies, while thy hook
Spares the next swath and all its twined flowers:
And sometimes like a gleaner thou dost keep
Steady thy laden head across a brook;
Or by a cider-press, with patient look,
Thou watchest the last oozings hours by hours.

Where are the songs of Spring? Ay, where are they?
Think not of them, thou hast thy music too, –
While barred clouds bloom the soft-dying day,
And touch the stubble-plains with rosy hue;
Then in a wailful choir the small gnats mourn
Among the river sallows, borne aloft
Or sinking as the light wind lives or dies;
And full-grown lambs loud bleat from hilly bourn;
Hedge-crickets sing; and now with treble soft
The red-breast whistles from a garden-croft;
And gathering swallows twitter in the skies.

John Keats

Pied Beauty

Glory be to God for dappled things –
   For skies of couple-colour as a brinded cow;
      For rose-moles all in stipple upon trout that swim;
Fresh-firecoal chestnut-falls; finches' wings;
   Landscape plotted and pieced – fold, fallow, and
      plough;
      And áll trádes, their gear and tackle and trim.

All things counter, original, spare, strange;
   Whatever is fickle, freckled (who knows how?)
      With swift, slow; sweet, sour; adazzle, dim;
He fathers-forth whose beauty is past change:
   Praise him.

Gerard Manley Hopkins

4.

stress-beating

Every moment of our lives is governed by rhythm. As early as six weeks into gestation, the foetal heartbeat has established itself, and the subsequent development of the brain – and the emergence of consciousness – takes place to the ambient music of the heart's drumbeat. A small area in the top right-hand corner of the heart, known as the sinoatrial node, controls the heart rate. In response, the alternating contractions of the four chambers of the heart with the snapping shut of the valves at the entrance and exit of the ventricles direct the onward surge of blood, creating the unmistakeable *lub dub* sounds that are heard through the stethoscope.

Superimposed on this are other rhythms, generated by more external, or celestial, forces. There is the movement of the Earth, tilted on its axis, and the gravitational attraction of the Moon – as well as our planet's year-long waltz around the Sun; the 24-hour-long circadian rhythm that is present not just in humans but throughout the natural world; the weeks and the months and the years; the seasons – even the tides and the waves. Poetry takes its cue instinctively – and vitally – from this rhythmic dance of life.

Hearing a poem's rhythm, from the pulse of John Masefield's 'Sea Fever' to the grace of Lord Byron's night-walking beauty, becomes a way of regulating our own heart-beat. Very often, though not always, poems also create harmony and satisfaction through rhyme. When a poet gives us a well-known rhyme, it can be like a kind of homecoming. Even in sadness, the familiar meetings of Chidiock Tichborne's 'womb' and 'tomb', or the chime of Edward Thomas's 'light' and 'night', strike a reassuring note. Sometimes rhyme seems to act as a kind of salve. Wordsworth wrote that its music forms an enduring pattern, which helps us, in turn, to endure things.

Song from *Cymbeline*

Fear no more the heat o' the sun,
Nor the furious winter's rages;
Thou thy worldly task hast done,
Home art gone, and ta'en thy wages:
Golden lads and girls all must,
As chimney-sweepers, come to dust.

Fear no more the frown o' the great;
Thou art past the tyrant's stroke;
Care no more to clothe and eat;
To thee the reed is as the oak:
The sceptre, learning, physic, must
All follow this, and come to dust.

Fear no more the lightning flash,
Nor the all-dreaded thunder stone;
Fear not slander, censure rash;
Thou hast finished joy and moan:
All lovers young, all lovers must
Consign to thee, and come to dust.

No exorciser harm thee!
Nor no witchcraft charm thee!
Ghost unlaid forbear thee!
Nothing ill come near thee!

Quiet consummation have;
And renownèd be thy grave!

William Shakespeare

The Tiger

Tiger Tiger, burning bright,
In the forests of the night:
What immortal hand or eye,
Could frame thy fearful symmetry?

In what distant deeps or skies,
Burnt the fire of thine eyes?
On what wings dare he aspire?
What the hand, dare seize the fire?

And what shoulder, and what art,
Could twist the sinews of thy heart?
And when thy heart began to beat,
What dread hand? and what dread feet?

What the hammer? what the chain,
In what furnace was thy brain?
What the anvil? what dread grasp,
Dare its deadly terrors clasp!

When the stars threw down their spears
And watered heaven with their tears:
Did he smile his work to see?
Did he who made the Lamb make thee?

Tiger Tiger burning bright,
In the forests of the night:
What immortal hand or eye,
Dare frame thy fearful symmetry?

William Blake

She walks in beauty

She walks in beauty, like the night
    Of cloudless climes and starry skies;
And all that's best of dark and bright
    Meet in her aspect and her eyes:
Thus mellowed to that tender light
    Which heaven to gaudy day denies.

One shade the more, one ray the less,
    Had half impaired the nameless grace
Which waves in every raven tress,
    Or softly lightens o'er her face;
Where thoughts serenely sweet express
    How pure, how dear their dwelling-place.

And on that cheek, and o'er that brow,
    So soft, so calm, yet eloquent,
The smiles that win, the tints that glow,
    But tell of days in goodness spent,
A mind at peace with all below,
    A heart whose love is innocent!

Lord Byron

Break, break, break

Break, break, break,
   On thy cold grey stones, O Sea!
And I would that my tongue could utter
   The thoughts that arise in me.

O, well for the fisherman's boy,
   That he shouts with his sister at play!
O, well for the sailor lad,
   That he sings in his boat on the bay!

And the stately ships go on
   To their haven under the hill;
But O for the touch of a vanished hand,
   And the sound of a voice that is still!

Break, break, break
   At the foot of thy crags, O Sea!
But the tender grace of a day that is dead
   Will never come back to me.

Alfred, Lord Tennyson

My Bed Is a Boat

My bed is like a little boat;
　Nurse helps me in when I embark;
She girds me in my sailor's coat
　And starts me in the dark.

At night, I go on board and say
　Good night to all my friends on shore;
I shut my eyes and sail away
　And see and hear no more.

And sometimes things to bed I take,
　As prudent sailors have to do;
Perhaps a slice of wedding-cake,
　Perhaps a toy or two.

All night across the dark we steer;
　But when the day returns at last,
Safe in my room, beside the pier,
　I find my vessel fast.

Robert Louis Stevenson

Sea Fever

I must down to the seas again, to the lonely sea and the
    sky,
And all I ask is a tall ship and a star to steer her by;
And the wheel's kick and the wind's song and the white
    sail's shaking,
And a grey mist on the sea's face, and a grey dawn
    breaking.

I must down to the seas again, for the call of the running
    tide
Is a wild call and a clear call that may not be denied;
And all I ask is a windy day with the white clouds flying,
And the flung spray and the blown spume, and the
    sea-gulls crying.

I must down to the seas again, to the vagrant gypsy life,
To the gull's way and the whale's way where the wind's
    like a whetted knife;
And all I ask is a merry yarn from a laughing
    fellow-rover,
And quiet sleep and a sweet dream when the long trick's
    over.

John Masefield

The Passionate Shepherd to His Love

Come live with me and be my love,
And we will all the pleasures prove,
That valleys, groves, hills, and fields,
Woods, or steepy mountain yields.

And we will sit upon the rocks,
Seeing the shepherds feed their flocks,
By shallow rivers to whose falls
Melodious birds sing madrigals.

And I will make thee beds of roses
And a thousand fragrant posies,
A cap of flowers, and a kirtle
Embroidered all with leaves of myrtle;

A gown made of the finest wool
Which from our pretty lambs we pull;
Fair-linèd slippers for the cold,
With buckles of the purest gold;

A belt of straw and ivy buds,
With coral clasps and amber studs:
And if these pleasures may thee move,
Come live with me, and be my love.

The shepherds' swains shall dance and sing
For thy delight each May-morning:
If these delights thy mind may move,
Then live with me, and be my love.

Christopher Marlowe

My prime of youth is but a frost of cares

My prime of youth is but a frost of cares,
My feast of joy is but a dish of pain,
My crop of corn is but a field of tares,
And all my good is but vain hope of gain.
The day is gone and yet I saw no sun,
And now I live, and now my life is done.

The spring is past, and yet it hath not sprung,
The fruit is dead, and yet the leaves are green,
My youth is gone, and yet I am but young,
I saw the world, and yet I was not seen,
My thread is cut, and yet it was not spun,
And now I live, and now my life is done.

I sought my death and found it in my womb,
I looked for life and saw it was a shade,
I trod the earth and knew it was my tomb,
And now I die, and now I am but made.
The glass is full, and now the glass is run,
And now I live, and now my life is done.

Chidiock Tichborne
Written in the Tower of London
on the eve of his execution

Heaven

O who will show me those delights on high?
    Echo.   *I.*
Thou Echo, thou art mortal, all men know.
    Echo.   *No.*
Wert thou not born among the trees and leaves?
    Echo.   *Leaves.*
And are there any leaves, that still abide?
    Echo.   *Bide.*
What leaves are they? impart the matter wholly.
    Echo.   *Holy.*
Are holy leaves the Echo then of bliss?
    Echo.   *Yes.*
Then tell me, what is that supreme delight?
    Echo.   *Light.*
Light to the mind: what shall the will enjoy?
    Echo.   *Joy.*
But are there cares and business with the pleasure?
    Echo.   *Leisure.*
Light, joy, and leisure; but shall they persever?
    Echo.   *Ever.*

George Herbert

The Windhover

To Christ Our Lord

I caught this morning morning's minion, king-
   dom of daylight's dauphin, dapple-dawn-drawn
      Falcon, in his riding
   Of the rolling level underneath him steady air, and
      striding
High there, how he rung upon the rein of a wimpling
   wing
In his ecstasy! then off, off forth on swing,
   As a skate's heel sweeps smooth on a bow-bend: the
      hurl and gliding
   Rebuffed the big wind. My heart in hiding
Stirred for a bird, – the achieve of, the mastery of the
   thing.
Brute beauty and valour and act, oh, air, pride, plume,
   here
   Buckle! AND the fire that breaks from thee then, a
      billion
Times told lovelier, more dangerous, O my chevalier!

   No wonder of it: shéer plód makes plough down
      sillion
Shine, and blue-bleak embers, ah my dear,
   Fall, gall themselves, and gash gold-vermilion.

Gerard Manley Hopkins

Morning Has Broken

Morning has broken,
Like the first morning,
Blackbird has spoken
Like the first bird;
Praise for the singing,
Praise for the morning,
Praise for them springing
Fresh from the Word.

Sweet the rain's new fall,
Sunlit from heaven,
Like the first dewfall
On the first grass;
Praise for the sweetness,
Of the wet garden,
Sprung in completeness
Where His feet pass.

Mine is the sunlight,
Mine is the morning,
Born of the one light
Eden saw play;

Praise with elation,
Praise every morning,
God's re-creation
Of the new day.

Eleanor Farjeon

5.

remembering

In times of stress and distress, we may find comfort in thinking back on times of happiness: of being in love, of childhood, of family and friends. These poems of love and lyrics of memory can be, in their own way, spirit-lifting and restorative. Some of them remember and celebrate erotic love, while others remind us that the quieter joys of friendship may endure longer than the intensity of passion. Christina Rossetti in the lovely sonnet 'Remember' invokes the power of memory when a loved one has 'gone far away into the silent land'. For the philosopher, Ralph Waldo Emerson, memory is 'the cement' that holds our self together: 'it is the thread on which the beads of man are strung'.

Sometimes memory may make you feel, temporarily, unstrung. As he listens to a woman singing, music and words transport D. H. Lawrence 'back down the vista of years' to his childhood self, sitting under the piano in the tiny parlour of his humble family home. Past and present disconcertingly collide. But through his remembering tears, a richer, more layered sense of self emerges. Indeed, our layers of memory are so bound up with our sense of self that when conditions such as dementia cause memory loss, a vital part of identity begins to ebb away. Reconnecting with memories from the distant past – and from childhood – is one way of regaining control over the destructive effects of memory loss. Often, snatches of poetry and songs learned by heart in childhood are the few things that remain when all else seems forgotten. Poetic memory remains a powerful means of recapturing a sense of wonder and joy – and an expression of resistance.

At the end of the section you will find a long poem of memory, reflection and meditation: Samuel Taylor Coleridge watches over his sleeping child as he thinks back on his own childhood and prays for his little boy's future. Coleridge, like his great contemporary Wordsworth, knew the pain of losing a child: his son Berkeley died in infancy. A key image at the heart of the poem is that of a fluttering film of soot on the grate of a fire. In country lore, this was taken as a sign that a 'stranger' would soon visit. But Coleridge is visited by his own thoughts instead, first memory and then hope. This is one of the greatest meditative poems ever written, composed in a gentle, conversational five-beat rhythm, unrhymed, conversational, absorbed in the moment, seeming a poem more by accident than design, and yet full of beautiful natural imagery and profound reflection on human life.

Sonnet 30

When to the sessions of sweet silent thought
I summon up remembrance of things past,
I sigh the lack of many a thing I sought,
And with old woes new wail my dear time's waste:
Then can I drown an eye, unused to flow,
For precious friends hid in death's dateless night,
And weep afresh love's long since cancelled woe,
And moan the expense of many a vanished sight:
Then can I grieve at grievances foregone,
And heavily from woe to woe tell o'er
The sad account of fore-bemoanèd moan,
Which I new pay as if not paid before.
　　But if the while I think on thee, dear friend,
　　All losses are restored and sorrows end.

William Shakespeare

Piano

Softly, in the dusk, a woman is singing to me;
Taking me back down the vista of years, till I see
A child sitting under the piano, in the boom of the
    tingling strings
And pressing the small, poised feet of a mother who
    smiles as she sings.
In spite of myself, the insidious mastery of song
Betrays me back, till the heart of me weeps to belong
To the old Sunday evenings at home, with winter outside
And hymns in the cosy parlour, the tinkling piano our
    guide.
So now it is vain for the singer to burst into clamour
With the great black piano appassionato. The glamour
Of childish days is upon me, my manhood is cast
Down in the flood of remembrance, I weep like a child
    for the past.

D. H. Lawrence

The Echoing Green

The sun does arise,
And make happy the skies.
The merry bells ring
To welcome the Spring.
The sky-lark and thrush,
The birds of the bush,
Sing louder around,
To the bells' cheerful sound.
While our sports shall be seen
On the Echoing Green.

Old John, with white hair
Does laugh away care,
Sitting under the oak,
Among the old folk,
They laugh at our play,
And soon they all say:
'Such, such were the joys.
When we all girls & boys,
In our youth-time were seen,
On the Echoing Green.'

Till the little ones weary
No more can be merry
The sun does descend,
And our sports have an end:

Round the laps of their mothers,
Many sisters and brothers,
Like birds in their nest,
Are ready for rest;
And sport no more seen,
On the darkening Green.

William Blake

My Grandmother's Love Letters

There are no stars tonight
But those of memory.
Yet how much room for memory there is
In the loose girdle of soft rain.

There is even room enough
For the letters of my mother's mother,
Elizabeth,
That have been pressed so long
Into a corner of the roof
That they are brown and soft,
And liable to melt as snow.

Over the greatness of such space
Steps must be gentle.
It is all hung by an invisible white hair.
It trembles as birch limbs webbing the air.

And I ask myself:

'Are your fingers long enough to play
Old keys that are but echoes:
Is the silence strong enough
To carry back the music to its source
And back to you again
As though to her?'

Yet I would lead my grandmother by the hand
Through much of what she would not understand;
And so I stumble. And the rain continues on the roof
With such a sound of gently pitying laughter.

Hart Crane

Venetian Night

Her eyes in the darkness shone, in the twilight shed
By the gondola bent like the darkness over her head.
Softly the gondola rocked, lights came and went;
A white glove shone as her black fan lifted and leant
Where the silk of her dress, the blue of a bittern's wing,
Rustled against my knee, and, murmuring
The sweet slow hesitant English of a child,
Her voice was articulate laughter, her soul smiled.
Softly the gondola rocked, lights came and went;
From the sleeping houses a shadow of slumber leant
Over our heads like a wing, and the dim lagoon,
Rustling with silence, slumbered under the moon.
Softly the gondola rocked, and a pale light came
Over the waters, mild as a silver flame;
She lay back, thrilling with smiles, in the twilight shed
By the gondola bent like the darkness over her head;
I saw her eyes shine subtly, then close awhile:
I remember her silence, and, in the night, her smile.

Arthur Symons

Remember

Remember me when I am gone away,
    Gone far away into the silent land;
    When you can no more hold me by the hand,
Nor I half turn to go yet turning stay.
Remember me when no more day by day
    You tell me of our future that you planned:
    Only remember me; you understand
It will be late to counsel then or pray.
Yet if you should forget me for a while
    And afterwards remember, do not grieve:
    For if the darkness and corruption leave
    A vestige of the thoughts that once I had,
Better by far you should forget and smile
    Than that you should remember and be sad.

Christina Rossetti

Love and Friendship

Love is like the wild rose-briar,
Friendship like the holly-tree –
The holly is dark when the rose-briar blooms
But which will bloom most constantly?

The wild rose-briar is sweet in spring,
Its summer blossoms scent the air;
Yet wait till winter comes again
And who will call the wild-briar fair?

Then scorn the silly rose-wreath now
And deck thee with the holly's sheen,
That when December blights thy brow
He still may leave thy garland green.

Emily Brontë

To Time

Yes, gentle time, thy gradual, healing hand
Hath stolen from sorrow's grasp the envenomed dart;
Submitting to thy skill, my passive heart
Feels that no grief can thy soft power withstand;
And though my aching breast still heaves the sigh,
Though oft the tear swells silent in mine eye;
Yet the keen pang, the agony is gone;
Sorrow and I shall part; and these faint throes
Are but the remnant of severer woes:
As when the furious tempest is o'erblown,
And when the sky has wept its violence,
The opening heavens will oft let fall a shower,
The poor o'ercharged boughs still drops dispense,
And still the loaded streams in torrents pour.

Mary Tighe

Frost at Midnight

The frost performs its secret ministry,
Unhelped by any wind. The owlet's cry
Came loud – and hark, again! loud as before.
The inmates of my cottage, all at rest,
Have left me to that solitude, which suits
Abstruser musings: save that at my side
My cradled infant slumbers peacefully.
'Tis calm indeed! so calm, that it disturbs
And vexes meditation with its strange
And extreme silentness. Sea, hill, and wood,
This populous village! Sea, and hill, and wood,
With all the numberless goings-on of life,
Inaudible as dreams! the thin blue flame
Lies on my low-burnt fire, and quivers not;
Only that film, which fluttered on the grate,
Still flutters there, the sole unquiet thing.
Methinks, its motion in this hush of nature
Gives it dim sympathies with me who live,
Making it a companionable form,
Whose puny flaps and freaks the idling spirit
By its own moods interprets, every where
Echo or mirror seeking of itself,
And makes a toy of thought.

                              But O! how oft,
How oft, at school, with most believing mind,
Presageful, have I gazed upon the bars,
To watch that fluttering *stranger*! and as oft
With unclosed lids, already had I dreamt
Of my sweet birth-place, and the old church-tower,
Whose bells, the poor man's only music, rang
From morn to evening, all the hot Fair-day,
So sweetly, that they stirred and haunted me
With a wild pleasure, falling on mine ear
Most like articulate sounds of things to come!
So gazed I, till the soothing things, I dreamt,
Lulled me to sleep, and sleep prolonged my dreams!
And so I brooded all the following morn,
Awed by the stern preceptor's face, mine eye
Fixed with mock study on my swimming book:
Save if the door half opened, and I snatched
A hasty glance, and still my heart leaped up,
For still I hoped to see the *stranger's* face,
Townsman, or aunt, or sister more beloved,
My play-mate when we both were clothed alike!

   Dear Babe, that sleepest cradled by my side,
Whose gentle breathings, heard in this deep calm,
Fill up the interspersèd vacancies
And momentary pauses of the thought!

My babe so beautiful! It thrills my heart
With tender gladness, thus to look at thee,
And think that thou shalt learn far other lore,
And in far other scenes! For I was reared
In the great city, pent 'mid cloisters dim,
And saw nought lovely but the sky and stars.
But *thou*, my babe! shalt wander like a breeze
By lakes and sandy shores, beneath the crags
Of ancient mountain, and beneath the clouds,
Which image in their bulk both lakes and shores
And mountain crags: so shalt thou see and hear
The lovely shapes and sounds intelligible
Of that eternal language, which thy God
Utters, who from eternity doth teach
Himself in all, and all things in himself.
Great universal Teacher! he shall mould
Thy spirit, and by giving make it ask.

Therefore all seasons shall be sweet to thee,
Whether the summer clothe the general earth
With greenness, or the redbreast sit and sing
Betwixt the tufts of snow on the bare branch
Of mossy apple-tree, while the nigh thatch
Smokes in the sun-thaw; whether the eave-drops fall
Heard only in the trances of the blast,

Or if the secret ministry of frost
Shall hang them up in silent icicles,
Quietly shining to the quiet Moon.

Samuel Taylor Coleridge

6.

releasing

'There are times in life when people must know when *not* to let go' said the late Terry Pratchett. 'Balloons are designed to teach small children this.' The following poems explore the power of strong emotions, and the ways we release, or hold them close. Some are fast and furious. They work like verbal punchbags, where we witness a writer's need to lash out. Dylan Thomas's repeated rhymes assault the reader as he clings to the hope that his father might live, even as he lies dying: 'Rage, rage against the dying of the light.'

In a poem that is a joy to read aloud (or hear the author himself reading on YouTube), the British-Caribbean poet Linton Kwesi Johnson rages against injustice but also speaks of 'good courage' (his poem is a protest against the so-called 'Sus', short for 'suspected person', law, a reference to the use by police of the ancient Vagrancy Act as justification for 'stop and search', which led to disproportionate arrests of black youths in Britain in the late twentieth century).

George Herbert, a seventeenth-century poet-priest, offers another angry bid. This time God is the target, not man. Peace comes – but only after a 'fierce and wild' battle (filled with 'choler', punning on the ecclesiastical idea of a 'dog-collar'). Other poems are more surly than angry: Wyatt is a spurned lover past his sell-by-date; Edna St Vincent Millais broods in a bittersweet sonnet.

Contemporary guides to well-being focus on 'anger-management'. With breathing, relaxation and better communication, we may live, they argue, an 'anger-free life'. But perhaps before we can be anger-free, we might need to free the anger. These poems give negative emotions – the insult of rejection, the anger of loss, the confusion of selfhood – a composure, a dignity, and a peculiar kind of calm.

Clive James's 'Japanese Maple' releases something different. Facing terminal illness, James crafts a poem that speaks of death as 'a fading out'. He turns, with lines of astonishing beauty, to the vision of the new maple tree outside his window. First published in 2014, the poem became an instant classic, going 'viral' on Twitter. One of the things that struck readers worldwide was the beauty of this poetic farewell: the emotions of regret, loss and fear are played out formally through the measured use of the poetic line. Sometimes graceful, sometimes 'just uncomfortable', the strain of what he 'must do' is mirrored by the effort of reading the poem as it halts for a moment, as if to draw breath, and then 'lives on' in the next line: 'What I must do / Is live to see that'. The poem is wry, as well as sad. Life is seen as a perpetual game, with ever-changing players. The final rhyme, like a hand which clasps and then lets go, is a kind of release – a tribute to a 'world which shone / So brightly at the last, and then was gone'.

Do not go gentle

Do not go gentle into that good night,
Old age should burn and rave at close of day;
Rage, rage against the dying of the light.

Though wise men at their end know dark is right,
Because their words had forked no lightning they
Do not go gentle into that good night.

Good men, the last wave by, crying how bright
Their frail deeds might have danced in a green bay,
Rage, rage against the dying of the light.

Wild men who caught and sang the sun in flight,
And learn, too late, they grieved it on its way,
Do not go gentle into that good night.

Grave men, near death, who see with blinding sight
Blind eyes could blaze like meteors and be gay,
Rage, rage against the dying of the light.

And you, my father, there on that sad height,
Curse, bless, me now with your fierce tears, I pray.
Do not go gentle into that good night.
Rage, rage against the dying of the light.

Dylan Thomas

A Poison Tree

I was angry with my friend;
I told my wrath, my wrath did end.
I was angry with my foe:
I told it not, my wrath did grow.

And I watered it in fears,
Night and morning with my tears:
And I sunned it with smiles,
And with soft deceitful wiles.

And it grew both day and night.
Till it bore an apple bright.
And my foe beheld it shine,
And he knew that it was mine.

And into my garden stole,
When the night had veiled the pole;
In the morning glad I see;
My foe outstretched beneath the tree.

William Blake

Sonny's Lettah

(Anti-Sus Poem)

Brixtan Prison
Jebb Avenue
Landan south-west two
Inglan

Dear Mama,
Good Day.
I hope dat wen
deze few lines reach yu,
they may find yu in di bes af helt.

Mama,
I really don't know how fi tell yu dis,
cause I did mek a salim pramis
fi tek care a likkle Jim
an try mi bes fi look out fi him.

Mama,
I really did try mi bes,
but nondiles
mi sarry fi tell you seh
poor likkle Jim get arres.

It woz di miggle a di rush howah
wen evrybady jus a hosel an a bosel
fi goh home fi dem evenin showah;
mi an Jim stand up
waitin pan a bus,
nat cauzin no fus,
wen all af a sudden
a police van pull-up.

Out jump tree policeman,
di hole a dem carryin batan.
Dem waak straight up to mi an Jim.

One a dem hol awn to Jim
seh him tekin him in;
Jim tell him fi let goh a him
far him noh dhu notn
an him naw teef,
nat even a butn.
Jim start to wriggle
di police start to giggle.

Mama,
mek I tell yu whe dem dhu to Jim
Mama,
mek I tell yu whe dem dhu to him:

dem tump him in him belly
an it turn to jelly
dem lick him pan him back
and him rib get pap
dem lick him pan him hed
but it tuff like led
dem kick him in him seed
an it started to bleed

Mama,
I jus coudn stan-up deh
and noh dhu notn:

soh me jook one in him eye
an him started to cry
mi tump one in him mout
an him started to shout
mi kick one pan him shin
an him started to spin
mi tump him pan him chin
an him drap pan a bin

an crash
an ded.

Mama,
more policeman come dung
an beat mi to di grung;
dem charge Jim fi sus,
dem charge me fi murdah.

Mama,
don fret,
dont get depres
an doun-hearted.
Be af good courage
till I hear fram you.

I remain
your son,
Sonny.

Linton Kwesi Johnson

Carrion Comfort

Not, I'll not, carrion comfort, Despair, not feast on thee;
Not untwist – slack they may be – these last strands of
    man
In me ór, most weary, cry *I can no more.* I can;
Can something, hope, wish day come, not choose not to
    be.
But ah, but O thou terrible, why wouldst thou rude on
    me
Thy wring-world right foot rock? lay a lionlimb against
    me? scan
With darksome devouring eyes my bruisèd bones? and
    fan,
O in turns of tempest, me heaped there; me frantic to
    avoid thee and flee?

    Why? That my chaff might fly; my grain lie, sheer and
        clear.
Nay in all that toil, that coil, since (seems) I kissed the
    rod,
Hand rather, my heart lo! lapped strength, stole joy,
    would laugh, chéer.
Cheer whom though? the hero whose heaven-handling
    flung me, fóot tród

Me? or me that fought him? O which one? is it each one?
  That night, that year
Of now done darkness I wretch lay wrestling with (my
  God!) my God.

Gerard Manley Hopkins

The Collar

I struck the board, and cried, 'No more;
   I will abroad!
What? shall I ever sigh and pine?
My lines and life are free, free as the road,
Loose as the wind, as large as store.
   Shall I be still in suit?
Have I no harvest but a thorn
To let me blood, and not restore
What I have lost with cordial fruit?
   Sure there was wine
Before my sighs did dry it; there was corn
   Before my tears did drown it.
     Is the year only lost to me?
       Have I no bays to crown it,
No flowers, no garlands gay? All blasted?
   All wasted?
Not so, my heart; but there is fruit,
   And thou hast hands.
Recover all thy sigh-blown age
On double pleasures: leave thy cold dispute
Of what is fit and not. Forsake thy cage,
   Thy rope of sands,
Which petty thoughts have made, and made to thee
Good cable, to enforce and draw,
   And be thy law,
While thou didst wink and wouldst not see.

Away! take heed;
  I will abroad.
Call in thy death's-head there; tie up thy fears;
  He that forbears
  To suit and serve his need
  Deserves his load.'
But as I raved and grew more fierce and wild
  At every word,
Methought I heard one calling, *Child!*
  And I replied *My Lord.*

George Herbert

They flee from me

They flee from me that sometime did me seek
With naked foot, stalking in my chamber.
I have seen them gentle, tame, and meek,
That now are wild and do not remember
That sometime they put themself in danger
To take bread at my hand; and now they range,
Busily seeking with a continual change.

Thanked be fortune it hath been otherwise
Twenty times better; but once in special,
In thin array after a pleasant guise,
When her loose gown from her shoulders did fall,
And she me caught in her arms long and small;
Therewithall sweetly did me kiss
And softly said, 'Dear heart, how like you this?'

It was no dream: I lay broad waking.
But all is turned thorough my gentleness
Into a strange fashion of forsaking;
And I have leave to go of her goodness,
And she also, to use newfangleness.
But since that I so kindly am served
I would fain know what she hath deserved.

Thomas Wyatt

Time does not bring relief

Time does not bring relief; you all have lied
Who told me time would ease me of my pain!
I miss him in the weeping of the rain;
I want him at the shrinking of the tide;
The old snows melt from every mountain-side,
And last year's leaves are smoke in every lane;
But last year's bitter loving must remain
Heaped on my heart, and my old thoughts abide.
There are a hundred places where I fear
To go, – so with his memory they brim.
And entering with relief some quiet place
Where never fell his foot or shone his face
I say, 'There is no memory of him here!'
And so stand stricken, so remembering him.

Edna St Vincent Millay

Rain

Rain, midnight rain, nothing but the wild rain
On this bleak hut, and solitude, and me
Remembering again that I shall die
And neither hear the rain nor give it thanks
For washing me cleaner than I have been
Since I was born into solitude.
Blessed are the dead that the rain rains upon:
But here I pray that none whom once I loved
Is dying tonight or lying still awake
Solitary, listening to the rain,
Either in pain or thus in sympathy
Helpless among the living and the dead,
Like a cold water among broken reeds,
Myriads of broken reeds all still and stiff,
Like me who have no love which this wild rain
Has not dissolved except the love of death,
If love it be towards what is perfect and
Cannot, the tempest tells me, disappoint.

Edward Thomas

Japanese Maple

Your death, near now, is of an easy sort.
So slow a fading out brings no real pain.
Breath growing short
Is just uncomfortable. You feel the drain
Of energy, but thought and sight remain:

Enhanced, in fact. When did you ever see
So much sweet beauty as when fine rain falls
On that small tree
And saturates your brick back garden walls,
So many Amber Rooms and mirror halls?

Ever more lavish as the dusk descends
This glistening illuminates the air.
It never ends.
Whenever the rain comes it will be there,
Beyond my time, but now I take my share.

My daughter's choice, the maple tree is new.
Come autumn and its leaves will turn to flame.
What I must do
Is live to see that. That will end the game
For me, though life continues all the same:

Filling the double doors to bathe my eyes,
A final flood of colours will live on
As my mind dies,
Burned by my vision of a world that shone
So brightly at the last, and then was gone.

Clive James

7.

grieving

'On the bald street breaks the blank day'. This is what the poet Alfred Tennyson wrote as he tried to live without his beloved friend, Arthur Hallam, who, while engaged to Tennyson's sister, had died suddenly at the age twenty-two. The feeling of desolation we experience when someone we love dies often strips us of our words, leaving tears or silence, anger or questions. The few weeks of 'compassionate leave' that society gives us bear no relation to the long journey that many of us face as we try to live with our loss. The poems which follow try to give grief some breathing space, and to put the experience of loss into words – from Katherine Phillips's lament as she stares at an empty cradle, to Thomas Hardy's painfully dream-like song, as he calls out to his dead wife, and imagines her calling back, to A. E. Housman's regret that because his was a love that dared not speak its name, he never spoke the words of love that he yearned to express. Grief is a peculiarly private emotion, and one that masquerades as many others. It can feel like shame, or guilt, or apathy or near-madness. No one expression of sorrow maps neatly onto another. The uniqueness of each person's sorrow must always be respected. And yet a poem can provide a tremendous sense of letting go, of catharsis. To read of a mother's or father's or friend's or lover's grief in ages long past is to know that others have been through the same experience and come out the other side.

Bereavement is the most aching form of loss, but we grieve for many things. The end of a relationship, for example. In 'The Dong with the Luminous Nose' Edward Lear, a lonely homosexual Victorian poet and artist who struggled through epilepsy and depression, pulls off the extraordinary feat of simultaneously capturing the pained bewilderment of a deserted lover and the sheer arbitrariness, the absurdity, of love: the Dong and the Jumbly Girl are the unlikeliest of couples, but his anguish at her departure is no less heart-wrenching for that.

These poems don't just work through words. Each poet uses the blankness of the page's space as a way of communicating feelings that are beyond speech. Facing the death of his son, Ben Jonson asks, 'For why', only to confront the blankness of the poem's line-end. The final '– O' of Wilfred Owen's poem seems, in its stuttering hyphen and enclosed circle – to draw a picture of futility. Dwelling on the words of these poems, and on the spaces between them, may help to give us a little more time – and space – to grieve.

Dark House, from *In Memoriam A. H. H.*

Dark house, by which once more I stand
   Here in the long unlovely street,
   Doors, where my heart was used to beat
So quickly, waiting for a hand,

A hand that can be clasped no more –
   Behold me, for I cannot sleep,
   And like a guilty thing I creep
At earliest morning to the door.

He is not here; but far away
   The noise of life begins again,
   And ghastly thro' the drizzling rain
On the bald street breaks the blank day.

Alfred, Lord Tennyson

Child Born Dead

What ceremony can we fit
You into now? If you had come
Out of a warm and noisy room
To this, there'd be an opposite
For us to know you by. We could
Imagine you in lively mood.

And then look at the other side,
The mood drawn out of you, the breath
Defeated by the power of death.
But we have never seen you stride
Ambitiously the world we know.
You could not come and yet you go.

But there is nothing now to mar
Your clear refusal of our world.
Not in our memories can we mould
You or distort your character.
Then all our consolation is
That grief can be as pure as this.

Elizabeth Jennings

On My First Son

Farewell, thou child of my right hand, and joy;
My sin was too much hope of thee, loved boy.
Seven years tho' wert lent to me, and I thee pay,
Exacted by thy fate, on the just day.
O, could I lose all father now! For why
Will man lament the state he should envy?
To have so soon 'scaped world's and flesh's rage,
And if no other misery, yet age?
Rest in soft peace, and, asked, say, 'Here doth lie
Ben Jonson his best piece of poetry.'
For whose sake henceforth all his vows be such,
As what he loves may never like too much.

Ben Jonson

On the Death of my First and Dearest Child, Hector Philips, born the 23rd of April, and died the 2nd of May 1655

Twice forty months in wedlock I did stay,
Then had my vows crowned with a lovely boy.
And yet in forty days he dropped away;
O swift vicissitude of human joy!

I did but see him, and he disappeared,
I did but touch the rosebud, and it fell;
A sorrow unforeseen and scarcely feared,
So ill can mortals their afflictions spell.

And now (sweet babe) what can my trembling heart
Suggest to right my doleful fate or thee?
Tears are my muse, and sorrow all my art,
So piercing groans must be thy elegy.

Thus whilst no eye is witness of my moan,
I grieve thy loss (ah, boy too dear to live!)
And let the unconcernèd world alone,
Who neither will, nor can refreshment give.

An offering too for thy sad tomb I have,
Too just a tribute to thy early hearse;
Receive these gasping numbers to thy grave,
The last of thy unhappy mother's verse.

Katherine Phillips

Remembrance

Cold in the earth – and the deep snow piled above thee,
Far, far removed, cold in the dreary grave!
Have I forgot, my only Love, to love thee,
Severed at last by Time's all-severing wave?

Now, when alone, do my thoughts no longer hover
Over the mountains, on that northern shore,
Resting their wings where heath and fern-leaves cover
Thy noble heart forever, ever more?

Cold in the earth – and fifteen wild Decembers,
From those brown hills, have melted into spring:
Faithful, indeed, is the spirit that remembers
After such years of change and suffering!

Sweet Love of youth, forgive, if I forget thee,
While the world's tide is bearing me along;
Other desires and other hopes beset me,
Hopes which obscure, but cannot do thee wrong!

No later light has lightened up my heaven,
No second morn has ever shone for me;
All my life's bliss from thy dear life was given,
All my life's bliss is in the grave with thee.

But, when the days of golden dreams had perished,
And even Despair was powerless to destroy,
Then did I learn how existence could be cherished,
Strengthened, and fed without the aid of joy.

Then did I check the tears of useless passion –
Weaned my young soul from yearning after thine;
Sternly denied its burning wish to hasten
Down to that tomb already more than mine.

And, even yet, I dare not let it languish,
Dare not indulge in memory's rapturous pain;
Once drinking deep of that divinest anguish,
How could I seek the empty world again?

Emily Brontë

The Voice

Woman much missed, how you call to me, call to me,
Saying that now you are not as you were
When you had changed from the one who was all to me,
But as at first, when our day was fair.

Can it be you that I hear? Let me view you, then,
Standing as when I drew near to the town
Where you would wait for me: yes, as I knew you then,
Even to the original air-blue gown!

Or is it only the breeze, in its listlessness
Travelling across the wet mead to me here,
You being ever dissolved to wan wistlessness,
Heard no more again far or near?

Thus I; faltering forward,
Leaves around me falling,
Wind oozing thin through the thorn from norward,
And the woman calling.

Thomas Hardy

Because I liked you better

Because I liked you better
   Than suits a man to say,
It irked you, and I promised
   I'd throw the thought away.

To put the world between us
   We parted, stiff and dry:
'Good-bye,' said you, 'forget me.'
   'I will, no fear,' said I.

If here, where clover whitens
   The dead man's knoll, you pass,
And no tall flower to meet you
   Starts in the trefoiled grass,

Halt by the headstone shading
   The heart no longer stirred,
And say the lad that loved you
   Was one that kept his word.

A. E. Housman

Futility

Move him into the sun –
Gently its touch awoke him once,
At home, whispering of fields unsown.
Always it woke him, even in France,
Until this morning and this snow.
If anything might rouse him now

The kind old sun will know.
Think how it wakes the seeds, –
Woke, once, the clays of a cold star.
Are limbs, so dear-achieved, are sides,
Full-nerved – still warm – too hard to stir?
Was it for this the clay grew tall?
– O what made fatuous sunbeams toil
To break earth's sleep at all?

Wilfred Owen

The Dong with a Luminous Nose

When awful darkness and silence reign
Over the great Gromboolian plain,
    Through the long, long wintry nights; –
When the angry breakers roar
As they beat on the rocky shore; –
    When Storm-clouds brood on the towering heights
Of the Hills of the Chankly Bore: –

Then, through the vast and gloomy dark,
There moves what seems a fiery spark,
    A lonely spark with silvery rays
    Piercing the coal-black night, –
    A Meteor strange and bright: –
Hither and thither the vision strays,
    A single lurid light.

Slowly it wanders, – pauses, – creeps, –
Anon it sparkles, – flashes and leaps;
And ever as onward it gleaming goes
A light on the Bong-tree stems it throws.
And those who watch at that midnight hour
From Hall or Terrace, or lofty Tower,
Cry, as the wild light passes along, –

'The Dong! – the Dong!
'The wandering Dong through the forest goes!
'The Dong! the Dong!
'The Dong with a luminous Nose!'

Long years ago
The Dong was happy and gay,
Till he fell in love with a Jumbly Girl
Who came to those shores one day,
For the Jumblies came in a sieve, they did, –
Landing at eve near the Zemmery Fidd
Where the Oblong Oysters grow,
And the rocks are smooth and gray.
And all the woods and the valleys rang
With the Chorus they daily and nightly sang, –
'Far and few, far and few,
Are the lands where the Jumblies live;
Their heads are green, and their hands are blue
And they went to sea in a sieve.'

Happily, happily passed those days!
While the cheerful Jumblies staid;
They danced in circlets all night long,
To the plaintive pipe of the lively Dong,
In moonlight, shine, or shade.

For day and night he was always there
By the side of the Jumbly Girl so fair,
With her sky-blue hands, and her sea-green hair.
Till the morning came of that hateful day
When the Jumblies sailed in their sieve away,
And the Dong was left on the cruel shore
Gazing – gazing for evermore, –
Ever keeping his weary eyes on
That pea-green sail on the far horizon, –
Singing the Jumbly Chorus still
As he sat all day on the grassy hill, –
    'Far and few, far and few,
    Are the lands where the Jumblies live;
    Their heads are green, and their hands are blue
    And they went to sea in a sieve.'

But when the sun was low in the West,
    The Dong arose and said; –
– 'What little sense I once possessed
    'Has quite gone out of my head!' –
And since that day he wanders still
By lake or forest, marsh and hill,
Singing – 'O somewhere, in valley or plain
'Might I find my Jumbly Girl again!

'For ever I'll seek by lake and shore
'Till I find my Jumbly Girl once more!'

   Playing a pipe with silvery squeaks,
   Since then his Jumbly Girl he seeks,
   And because by night he could not see,
   He gathered the bark of the Twangum Tree
   On the flowery plain that grows.
   And he wove him a wondrous Nose, –
   A Nose as strange as a Nose could be!
Of vast proportions and painted red,
And tied with cords to the back of his head.
   – In a hollow rounded space it ended
   With a luminous Lamp within suspended,
   All fenced about
   With a bandage stout
   To prevent the wind from blowing it out; –
   And with holes all round to send the light,
   In gleaming rays on the dismal night.

And now each night, and all night long,
Over those plains still roams the Dong;
And above the wall of the Chimp and Snipe
You may hear the squeak of his plaintive pipe

While ever he seeks, but seeks in vain
To meet with his Jumbly Girl again;
Lonely and wild – all night he goes, –
The Dong with a luminous Nose!
And all who watch at the midnight hour,
From Hall or Terrace, or lofty Tower,
Cry, as they trace the Meteor bright,
Moving along through the dreary night, –
   'This is the hour when forth he goes,
   'The Dong with a luminous Nose!
   'Yonder – over the plain he goes,
   'He goes!
   'He goes;
   'The Dong with a luminous Nose!'

Edward Lear

A slumber did my spirit seal

A slumber did my spirit seal;
   I had no human fears:
She seemed a thing that could not feel
   The touch of earthly years.

No motion has she now, no force;
   She neither hears nor sees;
Rolled round in earth's diurnal course,
   With rocks, and stones, and trees.

William Wordsworth

8.

feeling alone

In 1841, a middle-aged farm labourer called John Clare escaped from a lunatic asylum, driven by homesickness to find his childhood love. His mind, he wrote, was as much of a 'hell of a Madhouse' as the asylum itself. Clare's poem, 'I am', was written in another asylum a few years later. It describes a process of mental breakdown where 'friends forsake' him 'like a memory lost'. He is, he writes, the 'self-consumer' of his woes, and the poem turns inwards, as if consuming itself, and outwards into the blank page space. Clare's poem becomes, in its own way, 'like vapours tossed / Into the nothingness', as the sentence itself spans the void between two stanzas. Does Clare think he is sad, bad, bereft, or plain mad? The answer, like the title, is left hanging in thin air. It is a poem that gives voice to a self in the depths of mental pain, searching for solace.

Today, there's much discussion about the value of 'empathy' – the idea that we might recognize the feelings of others, and, to a certain degree share their emotions – and in doing so, reach out beyond the closed circle of selfhood. However, the pain of depression resists easy comprehension. Depressive pain – which can range from brief spells of what used to be called melancholy, to long periods of profound illness – is characterized by a kind of invisible wall, which blocks, rather than invites, companionship.

This section of the anthology follows Clare's poem with a sequence of meditations by poets who suffered from depression (and there have been many): Emily Dickinson, Gerard Manley Hopkins, Edward Thomas, Charlotte Mew. Their writings are distinct in tone. We have Dickinson's halting beauty; Hopkins' dramatic verbal contortions; Thomas's composed and musical despair; Mew's sense of claustrophobic terror. But they share something beyond words. These poems are unified by their strong rhythm. Pulsing like a heartbeat, their poetry bears witness to the spirit of endurance of all those who confront what we might call the dark night of the soul. To sense these rhythms we need to read these poems with something other than our minds and intellect – these poems ask for feeling.

I am

I am – yet what I am none cares or knows;
My friends forsake me like a memory lost:
I am the self-consumer of my woes –
They rise and vanish in oblivious host,
Like shadows in love's frenzied stifled throes
And yet I am, and live – like vapours tossed

Into the nothingness of scorn and noise,
Into the living sea of waking dreams,
Where there is neither sense of life or joys,
But the vast shipwreck of my life's esteems;
Even the dearest that I loved the best
Are strange – nay, rather, stranger than the rest.

I long for scenes where man hath never trod
A place where woman never smiled or wept
There to abide with my Creator, God,
And sleep as I in childhood sweetly slept,
Untroubling and untroubled where I lie
The grass below – above the vaulted sky.

John Clare

I Am the Song

I am the song that sings the bird.
I am the leaf that grows the land.
I am the tide that moves the moon.
I am the stream that halts the sand.
I am the cloud that drives the storm.
I am the earth that lights the sun.
I am the fire that strikes the stone.
I am the clay that shapes the hand.
I am the word that speaks the man.

Charles Causley

No worst, there is none

No worst, there is none. Pitched past pitch of grief,
More pangs will, schooled at forepangs, wilder wring.
Comforter, where, where is your comforting?
Mary, mother of us, where is your relief?
My cries heave, herds-long; huddle in a main, a chief
Woe, wórld-sorrow; on an áge-old anvil wince and sing –
Then lull, then leave off. Fury had shrieked 'No ling-
ering! Let me be fell: force I must be brief.'

  O the mind, mind has mountains; cliffs of fall
Frightful, sheer, no-man-fathomed. Hold them cheap
May who ne'er hung there. Nor does long our small
Durance deal with that steep or deep. Here! creep,
Wretch, under a comfort serves in a whirlwind: all
Life death does end and each day dies with sleep.

Gerard Manley Hopkins

I felt a Funeral, in my Brain

I felt a Funeral, in my Brain,
And Mourners to and fro
Kept treading – treading – till it seemed
That Sense was breaking through –

And when they all were seated,
A Service, like a Drum –
Kept beating – beating – till I thought
My mind was going numb –

And then I heard them lift a Box
And creak across my Soul
With those same Boots of Lead, again,
Then Space – began to toll,

As all the Heavens were a Bell,
And Being, but an Ear,
And I, and Silence, some strange Race,
Wrecked, solitary, here –

And then a Plank in Reason, broke,
And I dropped down, and down –
And hit a World, at every plunge,
And Finished knowing – then –

Emily Dickinson

Melancholy

The rain and wind, the rain and wind, raved endlessly.
On me the Summer storm, and fever, and melancholy
Wrought magic, so that if I feared the solitude
Far more I feared all company: too sharp, too rude,
Had been the wisest or the dearest human voice.
What I desired I knew not, but whate'er my choice
Vain it must be, I knew. Yet naught did my despair
But sweeten the strange sweetness, while through the
   wild air
All day long I heard a distant cuckoo calling
And, soft as dulcimers, sounds of near water falling,
And, softer, and remote as if in history,
Rumours of what had touched my friends, my foes, or
   me.

Edward Thomas

It was not Death, for I stood up

It was not Death, for I stood up,
And all the Dead, lie down –
It was not Night, for all the Bells
Put out their Tongues, for Noon.

It was not Frost, for on my Flesh
I felt Siroccos – crawl –
Nor Fire – for just my marble feet
Could keep a Chancel, cool –

And yet, it tasted, like them all,
The Figures I have seen
Set orderly, for Burial
Reminded me, of mine –

As if my life were shaven,
And fitted to a frame,
And could not breathe without a key,
And 'twas like Midnight, some –

When everything that ticked – has stopped –
And space stares – all around –
Or Grisly frosts – first Autumn morns,
Repeal the Beating Ground –

But most, like Chaos – Stopless – cool –
Without a Chance, or spar –
Or even a Report of Land –
To justify – Despair.

Emily Dickinson

Rooms

I remember rooms that have had their part
In the steady slowing down of the heart.
The room in Paris, the room at Geneva,
The little damp room with the seaweed smell,
And that ceaseless maddening sound of the tide –
   Rooms where for good or for ill – things died.
But there is the room where we (two) lie dead,
Though every morning we seem to wake and might just
   as well seem to sleep again
   As we shall somewhere in the other quieter, dustier
     bed
   Out there in the sun – in the rain.

Charlotte Mew

The Call

From our low seat beside the fire
　　Where we have dozed and dreamed and watched
　　　the glow
　Or raked the ashes, stopping so
We scarcely saw the sun or rain
　Above, or looked much higher
Than this same quiet red or burned-out fire.
　　　To-night we heard a call,
　　　A rattle on the window-pane,
　　　A voice on the sharp air,
And felt a breath stirring our hair,
　A flame within us: Something swift and tall
　Swept in and out and that was all.
Was it a bright or a dark angel? Who can know?
　It left no mark upon the snow,
　　But suddenly it snapped the chain
　　Unbarred, flung wide the door
　　Which will not shut again;
　And so we cannot sit here any more.
　　　We must arise and go:
　　The world is cold without
　　And dark and hedged about
　With mystery and enmity and doubt,

But we must go
   Though yet we do not know
Who called, or what marks we shall leave upon the
snow.

Charlotte Mew

9.

living with uncertainty

People can weather many things. We can often face pain, or loss, or sudden change head on, and with stoicism. But, as psychologists have shown, it is the state of uncertainty that really raises the pulse, and threatens us most. It's the *not knowing*, or the *not knowing how to cope with not knowing*, which can, in the end, cause most stress and psychic damage. Poets know this too. John Keats, writing in a letter to his brother, coined a term for being happily in limbo. He called it 'negative capability' – a state 'of being in uncertainties, Mysteries, doubts, without any irritable reaching after fact and reason.'

Poems can provide a way for us to practise 'negative capability'. Sometimes we read a poem like Christina Rossetti's 'Winter' and find that we are not quite sure what it means. Sometimes an individual word in a poem is so richly ambiguous that we can't pin one single meaning down, or we can't decide on a poem's tone. Consider Thomas Hardy's 'At Castle Boterel', one of a sequence of poems written in memory of his first wife. Their marriage ended unhappily and after she died he felt the need to remember earlier, happier days: so are the poem's final words, 'Never again', spoken with sorrow or bitterness or with a kind of blankness? Or again, what is

W. B. Yeats's 'Wandering Aengus' doing in the woods and why? We might find such uncertainties irritating, blaming ourselves, or the poet, for the lack of clarity. But managing to cope with these poems' deliberate inconclusiveness 'without any irritable reaching after fact or reason' can be a way of rehearsing our response to life's tougher questions. With some of these poems, as with life, we just have to wait it out.

With others, there is a sense of resolution. Matthew Arnold in 'Dover Beach', begun during his honeymoon, clings on to love at a time when the old religious certainties were disappearing with the advance of scientific under-standing during the Victorian era. Les Murray, writing in Australia in our own time, accepts that it is our own mental restlessness ('the talking mind') that questions 'the meaning of existence'. 'Trees, planets, rivers, time', by contrast, 'know nothing else. They express it / moment by moment as the universe'.

Out in the Dark

Out in the dark over the snow
The fallow fawns invisible go
With the fallow doe;
And the winds blow
Fast as the stars are slow.

Stealthily the dark haunts round
And, when the lamp goes, without sound
At a swifter bound
Than the swiftest hound,
Arrives, and all else is drowned;

And star and I and wind and deer,
Are in the dark together, – near,
Yet far, – and fear
Drums on my ear
In that sage company drear.

How weak and little is the light,
All the universe of sight,
Love and delight,
Before the might,
If you love it not, of night.

Edward Thomas

The Way through the Woods

They shut the road through the woods
Seventy years ago.
Weather and rain have undone it again,
And now you would never know
There was once a road through the woods
Before they planted the trees.
It is underneath the coppice and heath
And the thin anemones.
Only the keeper sees
That, where the ring-dove broods,
And the badgers roll at ease,
There was once a road through the woods.

Yet, if you enter the woods
Of a summer evening late,
When the night-air cools on the trout-ringed pools
Where the otter whistles his mate,
(They fear not men in the woods,
Because they see so few.)
You will hear the beat of a horse's feet,
And the swish of a skirt in the dew,
Steadily cantering through
The misty solitudes,
As though they perfectly knew

The old lost road through the woods ...
But there is no road through the woods.

Rudyard Kipling

Winter: My Secret

I tell my secret? No indeed, not I;
Perhaps some day, who knows?
But not today; it froze, and blows and snows,
And you're too curious: fie!
You want to hear it? well:
Only, my secret's mine, and I won't tell.

Or, after all, perhaps there's none:
Suppose there is no secret after all,
But only just my fun.
Today's a nipping day, a biting day;
In which one wants a shawl,
A veil, a cloak, and other wraps:
I cannot ope to everyone who taps,
And let the draughts come whistling thro' my hall;
Come bounding and surrounding me,
Come buffeting, astounding me,
Nipping and clipping thro' my wraps and all.
I wear my mask for warmth: who ever shows
His nose to Russian snows
To be pecked at by every wind that blows?
You would not peck? I thank you for good will,
Believe, but leave the truth untested still.

Spring's an expansive time: yet I don't trust
March with its peck of dust,
Nor April with its rainbow-crowned brief showers,
Nor even May, whose flowers
One frost may wither thro' the sunless hours.

Perhaps some languid summer day,
When drowsy birds sing less and less,
And golden fruit is ripening to excess,
If there's not too much sun nor too much cloud,
And the warm wind is neither still nor loud,
Perhaps my secret I may say,
Or you may guess.

Christina Rossetti

At Castle Boterel

As I drive to the junction of lane and highway,
And the drizzle bedrenches the waggonette,
I look behind at the fading byway,
And see on its slope, now glistening wet,
Distinctly yet

Myself and a girlish form benighted
In dry March weather. We climb the road
Beside a chaise. We had just alighted
To ease the sturdy pony's load
When he sighed and slowed.

What we did as we climbed, and what we talked of
Matters not much, nor to what it led, –
Something that life will not be balked of
Without rude reason till hope is dead,
And feeling fled.

It filled but a minute. But was there ever
A time of such quality, since or before,
In that hill's story? To one mind never,
Though it has been climbed, foot-swift, foot-sore,
By thousands more.

Primaeval rocks form the road's steep border,
And much have they faced there, first and last,
Of the transitory in Earth's long order;
But what they record in colour and cast
Is – that we two passed.

And to me, though Time's unflinching rigour,
In mindless rote, has ruled from sight
The substance now, one phantom figure
Remains on the slope, as when that night
Saw us alight.

I look and see it there, shrinking, shrinking,
I look back at it amid the rain
For the very last time; for my sand is sinking,
And I shall traverse old love's domain
Never again.

Thomas Hardy

The Song of Wandering Aengus

I went out to the hazel wood,
Because a fire was in my head,
And cut and peeled a hazel wand,
And hooked a berry to a thread;
And when white moths were on the wing,
And moth-like stars were flickering out,
I dropped the berry in a stream
And caught a little silver trout.

When I had laid it on the floor
I went to blow the fire a-flame,
But something rustled on the floor,
And someone called me by my name:
It had become a glimmering girl
With apple blossom in her hair
Who called me by my name and ran
And faded through the brightening air.

Though I am old with wandering
Through hollow lands and hilly lands,
I will find out where she has gone,
And kiss her lips and take her hands;

And walk among long dappled grass,
And pluck till time and times are done,
The silver apples of the moon,
The golden apples of the sun.

W. B. Yeats

There's a certain Slant of light

There's a certain Slant of light,
Winter Afternoons –
That oppresses, like the Heft
Of Cathedral Tunes –

Heavenly Hurt, it gives us –
We can find no scar,
But internal difference –
Where the Meanings, are –

None may teach it – Any –
'Tis the seal Despair –
An imperial affliction
Sent us of the Air –

When it comes, the Landscape listens –
Shadows – hold their breath –
When it goes, 'tis like the Distance
On the look of Death –

Emily Dickinson

Dover Beach

The sea is calm tonight.
The tide is full, the moon lies fair
Upon the straits; on the French coast the light
Gleams and is gone; the cliffs of England stand,
Glimmering and vast, out in the tranquil bay.
Come to the window, sweet is the night-air!
Only, from the long line of spray
Where the sea meets the moon-blanched land,
Listen! you hear the grating roar
Of pebbles which the waves draw back, and fling,
At their return, up the high strand,
Begin, and cease, and then again begin,
With tremulous cadence slow, and bring
The eternal note of sadness in.

Sophocles long ago
Heard it on the Ægean, and it brought
Into his mind the turbid ebb and flow
Of human misery; we
Find also in the sound a thought,
Hearing it by this distant northern sea.

The Sea of Faith
Was once, too, at the full, and round earth's shore

Lay like the folds of a bright girdle furled.
But now I only hear
Its melancholy, long, withdrawing roar,
Retreating, to the breath
Of the night-wind, down the vast edges drear
And naked shingles of the world.

Ah, love, let us be true
To one another! for the world, which seems
To lie before us like a land of dreams,
So various, so beautiful, so new,
Hath really neither joy, nor love, nor light,
Nor certitude, nor peace, nor help for pain;
And we are here as on a darkling plain
Swept with confused alarms of struggle and flight,
Where ignorant armies clash by night.

Matthew Arnold

The Meaning of Existence

Everything except language
knows the meaning of existence.
Trees, planets, rivers, time
know nothing else. They express it
moment by moment as the universe.

Even this fool of a body
lives it in part, and would
have full dignity within it
but for the ignorant freedom
of my talking mind.

Les Murray

No coward soul is mine

No coward soul is mine
No trembler in the world's storm-troubled sphere
I see Heaven's glories shine
And Faith shines equal arming me from Fear

O God within my breast
Almighty ever-present Deity
Life, that in me hast rest,
As I, Undying Life, have power in Thee

Vain are the thousand creeds
That move men's hearts, unutterably vain,
Worthless as withered weeds
Or idlest froth amid the boundless main

To waken doubt in one
Holding so fast by thy infinity,
So surely anchored on
The steadfast rock of Immortality.

With wide-embracing love
Thy spirit animates eternal years
Pervades and broods above,
Changes, sustains, dissolves, creates and rears

Though earth and moon were gone
And suns and universes ceased to be
And Thou wert left alone
Every Existence would exist in Thee

There is not room for Death
Nor atom that his might could render void
Since thou art Being and Breath
And what thou art may never be destroyed.

Emily Brontë

10.

moving on

The sun rises on the morning after the dark night of the soul. Life goes on. We may look back on the past with sorrow or joy, regret or fondness, but we have to move forward. In the course of any human life, there is a perpetual temptation to look back on what might have been, or to wonder what might have happened if we had gone down what Robert Frost calls 'the road not taken.'

Being told to 'move on', to 'get over it', or to 'pull our socks up' is often less than helpful. But many of these poems remind us that physical motion – putting on our actual socks and boots and walking down a road not yet taken – can be a great healer. There is a lot to be said for slipping an anthology of poetry in your pocket, going on a long walk, and periodically stopping to read some of these poems. Preferably aloud (if you are alone, or not feeling too self-conscious).

Some of these poets, like Housman, make a point of lingering, looking back at the 'land of lost content'. Others travel more decisively, showing how we might move on by framing our feelings in a different way. Using a series of remarkable comparisons, John Donne's 'A Valediction Forbidding Mourning' offers a Renaissance version of what we now call Cognitive Behavioural Therapy, or CBT. A lover's parting, Donne argues, can be a positive thing. Separation is not a 'breach', but an 'expansion', like 'gold to aery thinness beat'. Pain is spun, through poetry, into something glittering and precious.

In a particularly moving poem at the end of this section, William Wordsworth writes about his feelings in the aftermath of the death of his young daughter. One day, out on a walk, he is 'surprised by joy'. He doesn't say what has lifted his heart – it doesn't matter whether it's dappled sunlight, a frisking lamb or a rainbow in the sky. He turns to share the joy with his little girl, then he remembers that she is no longer alive to share it. And then he feels guilty at the very fact of experiencing a moment of joy when she is dead. But no one would want a survivor to grieve for ever: there is a time for moving on, for recognizing that, whatever we have endured, we can still – in time – be surprised by joy.

The Road Not Taken

Two roads diverged in a yellow wood,
And sorry I could not travel both
And be one traveler, long I stood
And looked down one as far as I could
To where it bent in the undergrowth;

Then took the other, as just as fair,
And having perhaps the better claim,
Because it was grassy and wanted wear;
Though as for that the passing there
Had worn them really about the same,

And both that morning equally lay
In leaves no step had trodden black.
Oh, I kept the first for another day!
Yet knowing how way leads on to way,
I doubted if I should ever come back.

I shall be telling this with a sigh
Somewhere ages and ages hence:
Two roads diverged in a wood, and I –
I took the one less traveled by,
And that has made all the difference.

Robert Frost

Into my heart an air that kills,
from *A Shropshire Lad*

Into my heart an air that kills
From yon far country blows:
What are those blue remembered hills,
What spires, what farms are those?

That is the land of lost content,
I see it shining plain,
The happy highways where I went
And cannot come again.

A. E. Housman

What lips my lips have kissed

What lips my lips have kissed, and where, and why,
I have forgotten, and what arms have lain
Under my head till morning; but the rain
Is full of ghosts tonight, that tap and sigh
Upon the glass and listen for reply,
And in my heart there stirs a quiet pain
For unremembered lads that not again
Will turn to me at midnight with a cry.
Thus in the winter stands the lonely tree,
Nor knows what birds have vanished one by one,
Yet knows its boughs more silent than before:
I cannot say what loves have come and gone,
I only know that summer sang in me
A little while, that in me sings no more.

Edna St Vincent Millay

The Wild Swans at Coole

The trees are in their autumn beauty,
The woodland paths are dry,
Under the October twilight the water
Mirrors a still sky;
Upon the brimming water among the stones
Are nine-and-fifty swans.

The nineteenth autumn has come upon me
Since I first made my count;
I saw, before I had well finished,
All suddenly mount
And scatter wheeling in great broken rings
Upon their clamorous wings.

I have looked upon those brilliant creatures,
And now my heart is sore.
All's changed since I, hearing at twilight,
The first time on this shore,
The bell-beat of their wings above my head,
Trod with a lighter tread.

Unwearied still, lover by lover,
They paddle in the cold
Companionable streams or climb the air;
Their hearts have not grown old;

Passion or conquest, wander where they will,
Attend upon them still.

But now they drift on the still water,
Mysterious, beautiful;
Among what rushes will they build,
By what lake's edge or pool
Delight men's eyes when I awake some day
To find they have flown away?

W. B. Yeats

Crossing the Bar

Sunset and evening star,
   And one clear call for me!
And may there be no moaning of the bar,
   When I put out to sea,

   But such a tide as moving seems asleep,
   Too full for sound and foam,
When that which drew from out the boundless deep
   Turns again home.

   Twilight and evening bell,
   And after that the dark!
And may there be no sadness of farewell,
   When I embark;

   For tho' from out our bourne of Time and Place
   The flood may bear me far,
I hope to see my Pilot face to face
   When I have crost the bar.

Alfred, Lord Tennyson

A Valediction Forbidding Mourning

As virtuous men pass mildly away,
    And whisper to their souls to go,
Whilst some of their sad friends do say
    The breath goes now, and some say, No:

So let us melt, and make no noise,
    No tear-floods, nor sigh-tempests move;
'Twere profanation of our joys
    To tell the laity our love.

Moving of th' earth brings harms and fears,
    Men reckon what it did, and meant;
But trepidation of the spheres,
    Though greater far, is innocent.

Dull sublunary lovers' love
    (Whose soul is sense) cannot admit
Absence, because it doth remove
    Those things which elemented it.

But we by a love so much refined,
    That our selves know not what it is,
Inter-assurèd of the mind,
    Care less, eyes, lips, and hands to miss.

Our two souls therefore, which are one,
　　Though I must go, endure not yet
A breach, but an expansion,
　　Like gold to airy thinness beat.

If they be two, they are two so
　　As stiff twin compasses are two;
Thy soul, the fixed foot, makes no show
　　To move, but doth, if the other do.

And though it in the centre sit,
　　Yet when the other far doth roam,
It leans and hearkens after it,
　　And grows erect, as that comes home.

Such wilt thou be to me, who must,
　　Like th' other foot, obliquely run;
Thy firmness makes my circle just,
　　And makes me end where I begun.

John Donne

From Ecclesiastes, 3: 1–15

To every thing there is a season, and a time to every
    purpose under the heaven:
A time to be born, and a time to die; a time to plant, and
    a time to pluck up that which is planted;
A time to kill, and a time to heal; a time to break down,
    and a time to build up;
A time to weep, and a time to laugh; a time to mourn,
    and a time to dance;
A time to cast away stones, and a time to gather stones
    together; a time to embrace, and a time to refrain
    from embracing;
A time to get, and a time to lose; a time to keep, and a
    time to cast away;
A time to rend, and a time to sew; a time to keep silence,
    and a time to speak;
A time to love, and a time to hate; a time of war, and a
    time of peace.
What profit hath he that worketh in that wherein he
    laboureth?
I have seen the travail, which God hath given to the sons
    of men to be exercised in it.
He hath made every thing beautiful in his time: also he
    hath set the world in their heart, so that no man can
    find out the work that God maketh from the
    beginning to the end.

I know that there is no good in them, but for a man to
rejoice, and to do good in his life.
And also that every man should eat and drink, and enjoy
the good of all his labour, it is the gift of God.
I know that, whatsoever God doeth, it shall be for ever:
nothing can be put to it, nor any thing taken from it:
and God doeth it, that men should fear before him.
That which hath been is now; and that which is to be
hath already been; and God requireth that which is
past.

King James Bible

Surprised by Joy

Surprised by joy – impatient as the wind
I turned to share the transport – Oh! with whom
But thee, deep buried in the silent tomb,
That spot which no vicissitude can find?
Love, faithful love, recalled thee to my mind –
But how could I forget thee? Through what power,
Even for the least division of an hour,
Have I been so beguiled as to be blind
To my most grievous loss? – That thought's return
Was the worst pang that sorrow ever bore,
Save one, one only, when I stood forlorn,
Knowing my heart's best treasure was no more;
That neither present time, nor years unborn
Could to my sight that heavenly face restore.

William Wordsworth

11.

seizing the day

'Why', asks the poet Ben Jonson, 'should we defer our joys'?

There are many sensible reasons – from our work to our waistlines – why we might. But Jonson has a point. There's a lot to be said for thinking less about the future and more about the present – for enjoying the now. *Carpe diem*: seize the day, as the Roman poet Horace put it, at the climax of a famous ode.

A recent psychological study of wellbeing proved what the philosophers have been saying for years – that we are at our happiest when we are absorbed in what we are doing, rather than looking ahead, or casting our minds back. This doesn't mean we should begin living our lives without consequence, but that when people concentrate, absolutely, on what they are doing they are likely to feel better. Being 'in the now' can be tricky – sex and conversation might claim our attention more easily than tax returns and vacuuming – but we can, with practice, learn to be a little more present.

Some of this practice might come, simply, by reading a poem with our full attention. In this section, which begins with a new translation of the Horace poem, you will find poems about living in the moment: in the moment of love, or of imagined freedom (even when in prison), of enjoying a pet's playfulness (in the eighteenth century, the mentally ill poet Christopher Smart rejoiced in his cat Jeoffry). Some of this practice might come by allowing ourselves to think, like Edward Lear, or Lewis Carroll, a bit like a child again. When children play, they are living in the moment. So too are we when we laugh or even when we smile. Writing to the artist Holman Hunt, Lear talked of 'this ludicrously whirligig life which one suffers from first and laughs at afterwards'.

Carpe diem poems are traditionally associated with momentary gratification (often sexual) as a victory over time and mortality, as in Andrew Marvell's famous 'To His Coy Mistress', but they are also a means to count our blessings. When we are lucky enough to be in love or to know the depth of enduring love (read Anne Bradstreet's poem to her 'dear and loving husband', written in New England three and a half centuries ago), or when we laugh, or when we share what Hilaire Belloc calls 'the love of friends', we seize the day.

Ode

You really should not ask the question.
You're not allowed to know
When the end is coming
To me, to you.

Don't ask a fortune-teller.
You'll do much better, girl,
To treat the future like the past:
Forget it.

Whether you've many winters still to come,
Or whether your last will be this bitter one
That whips the cliff-eroding sea,
Be wise: have a drink and accept

That life is short, so hope should not be long.
In the few moments you've been listening to me,
Envious time has slid away.
Seize the day; don't trust tomorrow.

Horace, translated by Jonathan Bate

Song: to Celia

Come, my Celia, let us prove,
While we can, the sports of love;
Time will not be ours forever;
He at length our good will sever.
Spend not then his gifts in vain.
Suns that set may rise again;
But if once we lose this light,
'Tis with us perpetual night.
Why should we defer our joys?
Fame and rumour are but toys.
Cannot we delude the eyes
Of a few poor household spies,
Or his easier ears beguile,
So removèd by our wile?
'Tis no sin love's fruit to steal;
But the sweet thefts to reveal,
To be taken, to be seen,
These have crimes accounted been.

Ben Jonson

To Althea, from Prison

When Love with unconfinèd wings
   Hovers within my Gates,
And my divine *Althea* brings
   To whisper at the Grates;
When I lie tangled in her hair,
   And fettered to her eye,
The Gods that wanton in the Air,
   Know no such Liberty.

When flowing Cups run swiftly round
   With no allaying *Thames*,
Our careless heads with Roses bound,
   Our hearts with Loyal Flames;
When thirsty grief in Wine we steep,
   When Healths and draughts go free,
Fishes that tipple in the Deep
   Know no such Liberty.

When (like committed linnets) I
   With shriller throat shall sing
The sweetness, Mercy, Majesty,
   And glories of my King;
When I shall voice aloud how good
   He is, how Great should be,
Enlargèd Winds, that curl the Flood,
   Know no such Liberty.

Stone Walls do not a Prison make,
    Nor Iron bars a Cage;
Minds innocent and quiet take
    That for an Hermitage.
If I have freedom in my Love,
    And in my soul am free,
Angels alone that soar above,
    Enjoy such Liberty.

Richard Lovelace

To His Coy Mistress

Had we but world enough, and time,
This coyness, Lady, were no crime.
We would sit down and think which way
To walk and pass our long love's day.
Thou by the Indian Ganges' side
Shouldst rubies find: I by the tide
Of Humber would complain. I would
Love you ten years before the Flood,
And you should, if you please, refuse
Till the conversion of the Jews.
My vegetable love should grow
Vaster than empires, and more slow;
An hundred years should go to praise
Thine eyes and on thy forehead gaze;
Two hundred to adore each breast,
But thirty thousand to the rest;
An age at least to every part,
And the last age should show your heart.
For, Lady, you deserve this state,
Nor would I love at lower rate.
But at my back I always hear
Time's wingèd chariot hurrying near;
And yonder all before us lie
Deserts of vast eternity.
Thy beauty shall no more be found,
Nor, in thy marble vault, shall sound

My echoing song; then worms shall try
That long preserved virginity,
And your quaint honour turn to dust,
And into ashes all my lust:
The grave's a fine and private place,
But none, I think, do there embrace.
Now therefore, while the youthful hue
Sits on thy skin like morning dew,
And while thy willing soul transpires
At every pore with instant fires,
Now let us sport us while we may,
And now, like amorous birds of prey,
Rather at once our time devour
Than languish in his slow-chapped power.
Let us roll all our strength and all
Our sweetness up into one ball,
And tear our pleasures with rough strife
Through the iron gates of life:
Thus, though we cannot make our sun
Stand still, yet we will make him run.

Andrew Marvell

To My Dear and Loving Husband

If ever two were one, then surely we.
If ever man were loved by wife, then thee;
If ever wife was happy in a man,
Compare with me ye women if you can.
I prize thy love more than whole mines of gold,
Or all the riches that the East doth hold.
My love is such that rivers cannot quench,
Nor ought but love from thee give recompense.
Thy love is such I can no way repay;
The heavens reward thee manifold, I pray.
Then while we live, in love let's so persever,
That when we live no more we may live ever.

Anne Bradstreet

For I will consider my Cat Jeoffry, from *Jubilate Agno*

For I will consider my Cat Jeoffry.

For he is the servant of the Living God duly and daily serving him.

For at the first glance of the glory of God in the East he worships in his way.

For this is done by wreathing his body seven times round with elegant quickness.

For then he leaps up to catch the musk, which is the blessing of God upon his prayer.

For he rolls upon prank to work it in.

For having done duty and received blessing he begins to consider himself.

For this he performs in ten degrees.

For first he looks upon his forepaws to see if they are clean.

For secondly he kicks up behind to clear away there.

For thirdly he works it upon stretch with the forepaws extended.

For fourthly he sharpens his paws by wood.

For fifthly he washes himself.

For sixthly he rolls upon wash.

For seventhly he fleas himself, that he may not be interrupted upon the beat.

For eighthly he rubs himself against a post.

For ninthly he looks up for his instructions.

For tenthly he goes in quest of food.

For having considered God and himself he will consider his neighbour.

For if he meets another cat he will kiss her in kindness.

For when he takes his prey he plays with it to give it a chance.

For one mouse in seven escapes by his dallying.

For when his day's work is done his business more properly begins.

For he keeps the Lord's watch in the night against the adversary.

For he counteracts the powers of darkness by his electrical skin and glaring eyes.

For he counteracts the Devil, who is death, by brisking about the life.

For in his morning orisons he loves the sun and the sun loves him.

For he is of the tribe of Tiger.

Christopher Smart

from **Dedicatory Ode**

The wealth of youth, we spent it well
And decently, as very few can.
And is it lost? I cannot tell:
And what is more, I doubt if you can.

The question's very much too wide,
And much too deep, and much too hollow,
And learned men on either side
Use arguments I cannot follow.

They say that in the unchanging place,
Where all we loved is always dear,
We meet our morning face to face
And find at last our twentieth year …

They say (and I am glad they say)
It is so; and it may be so:
It may be just the other way,
I cannot tell. But this I know:

From quiet homes and first beginning,
Out to the undiscovered ends,
There's nothing worth the wear of winning,
But laughter and the love of friends.

Hilaire Belloc

The Owl and the Pussy-cat

The Owl and the Pussy-cat went to sea
   In a beautiful pea-green boat,
They took some honey, and plenty of money,
   Wrapped up in a five-pound note.
The Owl looked up to the stars above,
   And sang to a small guitar,
'O lovely Pussy! O Pussy, my love,
   What a beautiful Pussy you are,
     You are,
     You are!
What a beautiful Pussy you are!'

Pussy said to the Owl, 'You elegant fowl!
   How charmingly sweet you sing!
O let us be married! too long we have tarried:
   But what shall we do for a ring?'
They sailed away, for a year and a day,
   To the land where the Bong-Tree grows
And there in a wood a Piggy-wig stood
   With a ring at the end of his nose,
     His nose,
     His nose,
With a ring at the end of his nose.

'Dear Pig, are you willing to sell for one shilling
    Your ring?' Said the Piggy, 'I will.'
So they took it away, and were married next day
    By the Turkey who lives on the hill.
They dined on mince, and slices of quince,
    Which they ate with a runcible spoon;
And hand in hand, on the edge of the sand,
    They danced by the light of the moon,
        The moon,
        The moon,
They danced by the light of the moon.

Edward Lear

Jabberwocky

'Twas brillig, and the slithy toves
Did gyre and gimble in the wabe;
All mimsy were the borogoves,
And the mome raths outgrabe.

'Beware the Jabberwock, my son!
The jaws that bite, the claws that catch!
Beware the Jubjub bird, and shun
The frumious Bandersnatch!'

He took his vorpal sword in hand:
Long time the manxome foe he sought –
So rested he by the Tumtum tree,
And stood awhile in thought.

And as in uffish thought he stood,
The Jabberwock, with eyes of flame,
Came whiffling through the tulgey wood,
And burbled as it came!

One, two! One, two! and through and through
The vorpal blade went snicker-snack!
He left it dead, and with its head
He went galumphing back.

'And hast thou slain the Jabberwock?
Come to my arms, my beamish boy!
O frabjous day! Callooh! Callay!'
He chortled in his joy.

'Twas brillig, and the slithy toves
Did gyre and gimble in the wabe;
All mimsy were the borogoves,
And the mome raths outgrabe.

Lewis Carroll

The Last Laugh

I made hay while the sun shone.
My work sold.
Now, if the harvest is over
And the world cold,
Give me the bonus of laughter
As I lose hold.

John Betjeman

12.

positive thinking

The Roman poet Horace, who reminded us to 'seize the day', wrote that 'Patience makes lighter / What sorrow may not heal'.

Writing some two thousand years later, a young woman called Kate Gross also turned to poetry to lift a burden – and though she cared less for patience, she shared Horace's fiery belief in the power of the human mind.

Gross died of colon cancer in 2014. She was thirty-six, and left her husband and her two young twin boys behind. Before she died, she wrote a beautiful book called *Late Fragments*. Her final chapter turns to one of the poems that we include in the following section, W. E. Henley's 'Invictus':

To paraphrase the much-quoted words of a good, solid Victorian poet, you are the captain of your soul. What happens to you, uncontrollable or otherwise, isn't the important thing. What matters is simply how you *are* with it ... While I don't have a choice about cancer, or dying, I do have a choice. I have a choice about how I live with it and how I die ... You might expect to find me depleted, fretful, full of grief. You won't ... I assert that wonder and joy are more powerful than the sadness of a truncated life. I made this choice early on, returning to wry Jonathan Swift, who tells us to 'live all the days of our life'.

Such a sense of 'wonder and joy' endures through the poems that follow. From Henley's 'Invictus' (the title is the Latin for 'unconquered' – Henley wrote it following the amputation of both his legs) to George Herbert's 'Love', they describe how a mind may both accept its own strength, and admit its frailties. Together they speak of courage, and of grace. As our final section's first poem puts it, 'there is everything to look forward to'.

Or, in the words of the fourteenth-century anchoress and spiritual mystic Julian of Norwich – words which have often proved a mantra of comfort in times of trial – 'all shall be well, and all shall be well, and all manner of thing shall be well'.

Arrival

Not conscious
that you have been seeking
suddenly
you come upon it

the village in the Welsh hills
dust free
with no road out
but the one you came in by.

A bird chimes
from a green tree
the hour that is no hour
you know. The river dawdles
to hold a mirror for you
where you may see yourself
as you are, a traveler
with the moon's halo
above him, whom has arrived
after long journeying where he
began, catching this
one truth by surprise
that there is everything to look forward to.

R. S. Thomas

Invictus

Out of the night that covers me,
Black as the pit from pole to pole,
I thank whatever gods may be
For my unconquerable soul.

In the fell clutch of circumstance
I have not winced nor cried aloud.
Under the bludgeonings of chance
My head is bloody, but unbowed.

Beyond this place of wrath and tears
Looms but the Horror of the shade,
And yet the menace of the years
Finds and shall find me unafraid.

It matters not how strait the gate,
How charged with punishments the scroll,
I am the master of my fate,
I am the captain of my soul.

W. E. Henley

An Hymn to Humanity

Lo! for this dark terrestrial ball,
Forsakes his azure-paved hall,
A prince of heavenly birth!
Divine Humanity behold,
What wonders rise, what charms unfold
At his descent to earth!

The bosoms of the great and good
With wonder and delight he viewed,
And fixed his empire there:
Him close compressing to his breast,
The sire of gods and men addressed,
'My son, my heavenly fair!

'Descend to earth, there place thy throne;
To succour man's afflicted son,
Each human heart inspire:
To act in bounties unconfined,
Enlarge the close contracted mind,
And fill it with thy fire.'

Quick as the word, with swift career
He wings his course from star to star,

And leaves the bright abode.
The Virtue did his charms impart;
Their Gallowy! then thy raptured heart
Perceived the rushing God:

For then thy pitying eye did see
The languid muse in low degree,
Then, then at thy desire
Descended the celestial nine;
O'er me methought they deigned to shine,
And deigned to string my lyre.

Can Afric's muse forgetful prove?
Or can such friendship fail to move
A tender human heart?
Immortal Friendship laurel-crowned
The smiling Graces all surround
With every heavenly Art.

Phillis Wheatley
Dedicated to S. P. Gallowy, her editor
and friend (Wheatley was the first published
African-American woman poet)

To Music

You dear sweet Art, in many dismal hours
Where I've been bound by life's unruly course,
Then in my heart, a warmer love you have ignited:
You've carried me to a better, better world,
Yes, to a better, better world!

Oft comes a sigh, a holy chord from your harp strings
That sparks in me a vision, one I clearly see,
A glimpse of heaven, and the sight of better times before
   me,
I thank you for these things, you dear sweet Art,
For these things, my thanks to you.

Franz von Schober,
translated by Tom Potter

If –

If you can keep your head when all about you
    Are losing theirs and blaming it on you,
If you can trust yourself when all men doubt you,
    But make allowance for their doubting too;
If you can wait and not be tired by waiting,
    Or being lied about, don't deal in lies,
Or being hated, don't give way to hating,
    And yet don't look too good, nor talk too wise:

If you can dream – and not make dreams your master;
    If you can think – and not make thoughts your aim;
If you can meet with Triumph and Disaster
    And treat those two impostors just the same;
If you can bear to hear the truth you've spoken
    Twisted by knaves to make a trap for fools,
Or watch the things you gave your life to, broken,
    And stoop and build 'em up with worn-out tools:

If you can make one heap of all your winnings
    And risk it on one turn of pitch-and-toss,
And lose, and start again at your beginnings
    And never breathe a word about your loss;
If you can force your heart and nerve and sinew
    To serve your turn long after they are gone,
And so hold on when there is nothing in you
    Except the Will which says to them: 'Hold on!'

If you can talk with crowds and keep your virtue,
    Or walk with Kings – nor lose the common touch,
If neither foes nor loving friends can hurt you,
    If all men count with you, but none too much;
If you can fill the unforgiving minute
    With sixty seconds' worth of distance run,
Yours is the Earth and everything that's in it,
    And – which is more – you'll be a Man, my son!

Rudyard Kipling

A Psalm of Life

What the Heart of the Young Man Said to the Psalmist

Tell me not, in mournful numbers,
    Life is but an empty dream!
For the soul is dead that slumbers,
    And things are not what they seem.

Life is real! Life is earnest!
    And the grave is not its goal;
Dust thou art, to dust returnest,
    Was not spoken of the soul.

Not enjoyment, and not sorrow,
    Is our destined end or way;
But to act, that each to-morrow
    Find us farther than to-day.

Art is long, and Time is fleeting,
    And our hearts, though stout and brave,
Still, like muffled drums, are beating
    Funeral marches to the grave.

In the world's broad field of battle,
    In the bivouac of Life,
Be not like dumb, driven cattle!
    Be a hero in the strife!

Trust no Future, howe'er pleasant!
    Let the dead Past bury its dead!
Act, – act in the living Present!
    Heart within, and God o'erhead!

Lives of great men all remind us
    We can make our lives sublime,
And, departing, leave behind us
    Footprints on the sands of time;

Footprints, that perhaps another,
    Sailing o'er life's solemn main,
A forlorn and shipwrecked brother,
    Seeing, shall take heart again.

Let us, then, be up and doing,
    With a heart for any fate;
Still achieving, still pursuing,
    Learn to labor and to wait.

Henry Wadsworth Longfellow

O Me! O Life!

O me! O life! of the questions of these recurring,
Of the endless trains of the faithless, of cities filled with
    the foolish,
Of myself forever reproaching myself, (for who more
    foolish than I, and who more faithless?)
Of eyes that vainly crave the light, of the objects mean, of
    the struggle ever renewed,
Of the poor results of all, of the plodding and sordid
    crowds I see around me,
Of the empty and useless years of the rest, with the rest
    me intertwined,
The question, O me! so sad, recurring – What good amid
    these, O me, O life?

   Answer.
That you are here – that life exists and identity,
That the powerful play goes on, and you may contribute
    a verse.

Walt Whitman

Love

Love bade me welcome, yet my soul drew back,
    Guilty of dust and sin.
But quick-eyed Love, observing me grow slack
    From my first entrance in,
Drew nearer to me, sweetly questioning
    If I lacked anything.

'A guest,' I answered, 'worthy to be here';
    Love said, 'You shall be he.'
'I, the unkind, the ungrateful? ah my dear,
    I cannot look on thee.'
Love took my hand and smiling did reply,
    'Who made the eyes but I?'

'Truth, Lord, but I have marred them; let my shame
    Go where it doth deserve.'
'And know you not,' says Love, 'who bore the blame?'
    'My dear, then I will serve.'
'You must sit down,' says Love, 'and taste my meat.'
    So I did sit and eat.

George Herbert

Everything Is Going To Be All Right

How should I not be glad to contemplate
the clouds clearing beyond the dormer window
and a high tide reflected on the ceiling?
There will be dying, there will be dying,
but there is no need to go into that.
The poems flow from the hand unbidden
and the hidden source is the watchful heart;
the sun rises in spite of everything
and the far cities are beautiful and bright.
I lie here in a riot of sunlight
watching the day break and the clouds flying.
Everything is going to be all right.

Derek Mahon

afterword

This anthology is an extraordinary gift to the world. Between them, Jonathan Bate, Paula Byrne, Sophie Ratcliffe and Andrew Schuman combine the healing wisdom of literary scholarship and physical medicine. They remind us how people over the centuries have discovered through poetry a profound courage or even joy in the midst of their anguish, whether through the focused luminosity of haiku, the rhythm of a sonnet or the quiet beat of unrhymed verse.

The words and images in these poems can transform us. First, as the compilers of the anthology say, poetry can help clear the mind of other cares, replacing dark thoughts with more positive words and images. They enable us to turn towards themes other than those that are weighing us down right now. Here are poems that remind us to stop, to look again at the small things, to use all our senses, to notice things as if for the first time; the bright field, the Japanese maple, dappled things, a blessing in the air.

This 'coming to our senses' is enormously important, but the anthology does not stop there. Transformation of our own suffering sometimes asks us to go even deeper: to see and feel the tragedies experienced by others. So we hear the poets' own expressions of anger and grief and loneliness. We hear them putting into words feelings that are too painful for us to utter, and we are reminded that we are not alone in our sadness or fear. This sense of common humanity is the foundation of compassion; it allows an outpouring of love towards ourselves and others that may have been blocked.

The poems may touch us in unexpected ways too. Many of us carry burdens of which we are barely aware, but then find ourselves unaccountably in tears when reading the words of a poem. Even if we have not experienced the death of a child, the words of Ben Jonson or Elizabeth Jennings allow us to touch a universal sadness too deep for words, and to know a profound companionship in the midst of our own too frail mortality.

These classic poems are ideal for 'mindful reading'. What does this imply? From ancient times, mindfulness has been part of great spiritual traditions, cultivated by practices that show us how to make space for attentive presence, how to cultivate stillness in the midst of busyness. To do something mindfully means to do something with full awareness, whether it is walking, eating, sitting or breathing. Mindfulness is not about an ecstatic state of consciousness. It adds nothing to what is already here, but sees clearly – as if for the first time – what might have become hidden or taken for granted. It is walking, and knowing you are walking; eating, and knowing you are eating; sitting and breathing, and knowing you are sitting and breathing. It sounds simple, and it is; but it turns out to be extraordinarily difficult to do such a simple thing. For in our daily lives we are taught to rush around, to problem-solve and multi-task; and we become very proficient at it. This need not be a problem at all, if the task at hand requires such an approach; but we easily succumb to the danger of thinking that everything will yield to these 'means-ends' strategies. So when we meet a situation that cannot be solved in this way, such as mental anguish or physical illness in ourselves or our loved ones, we are at first puzzled and then we panic. We feel overwhelmed first by the situation and then by our own helplessness.

Mindfulness invites us to take a different approach. In cultivating greater moment-by-moment awareness, we learn how to let go of rushing. We learn how to sit quietly and wait for grace. The irony is that out of such gentle patience, wiser solutions often appear unbidden. This is why bringing mindfulness into the reading and reflection of these poems promises so much. If we can allow the healing power of stillness and the transformative power of poetry to work together, we may come to notice subtle changes in heart and mind, unexpected moments of appreciation; of coming home, of healing.

This anthology takes us on a journey, but allows us to start anywhere. Each section has its own introduction that is worth reading slowly and carefully; each sets the scene beautifully, making the intentions visible and speaking directly to the reader with gentleness and sensitivity. We are invited to slow down, to taste the words, as it were; to hear and to feel the rhythms; to sense the 'stresses and unstresses' – the presences and absences. Little by little, a wholly new way of being with and inside the words and images is offered to us.

There are specific suggestions about how to prepare for reading the poems we find here: focussing attention on our breathing, noticing its pace and regularity. This guidance echoes themes to be found in ancient meditative practices, which also begin with the body. In mindfulness instructions, we may be invited first to feel the ground under our feet, the weight of the body on the chair, the subtle sensations of the breath as it comes in and out of the body.

Why should starting with attending to the body be helpful? Because when emotions begin to overwhelm us, we automatically become drawn into the stories created by our thinking. These stories are often about the past or the future, haunting our minds with the worst sort of unanswerable speculation: *if only* and *what if.* There is no situation that is so bad that our thinking cannot make it worse. Just when we need all our resources to deal with the tragedies and chaos of our lives, thoughts such as 'This is all my fault – if only I had done something else' or 'What if I'm just not good enough?' drag us down even deeper into despair. Both ancient wisdom and modern psychological science tell us that it is enormously difficult to challenge these thoughts from within the realm of thinking itself. Shifting attention towards the physical sensations of the body, and then remaining for a while within them, allows the mind to enter a different mode, a mode of being rather than driven doing. This mindful mode does not ignore the chaos, yet is able to prioritise the present moment over re-living the past or pre-living the future. Here is a mode in which our desperate thoughts can be seen more clearly for what they are: mental events, coming and going in the mind.

Mindful reading of these poems encourages us to remain grounded as we read, so that a more holistic perspective becomes available to us. From this larger viewpoint, we may see more clearly how stressed we have been, how much we have been in the grip of a mood that coloured everything around us. From this clear seeing comes a release from the power that the mood had over us and perhaps the hint of a new feeling – that this condition too is somehow workable.

Jonathan Bate tells us in his introduction that these classic poems are 'intended for the waiting room, the sickbed, the sleepless night, the day when everything seems to be going wrong, the moment of respite'. He advises to keep it by our bed or stash it in our bag. This is wise advice. These poems will lie quietly, waiting to be brought to life by our reading of them, again and again.

May they give you heart, nourishing the deepest and most precious parts of who you are. May you find in them what you most need, whether this is peace, or love, or forgiveness, and may they give you courage to face what needs to be faced and to live the life that has so far been unlived.

Mark Williams

if you need help

There are many organizations ready to offer advice and help for those experiencing mental distress. A few are listed below:

Samaritans
  website: www.samaritans.org
  telephone: 116 123
  email: jo@samaritans.org

Mind, the mental health charity
  website: www.mind.org.uk
  telephone: 0300 123 3393
  email: info@mind.org.uk

Women's Aid
  website: www.womensaid.org.uk
  telephone: 0808 2000 247
  email: helpline@womensaid.org.uk

Childline
  website: www.childline.org.uk
  telephone: 0800 1111

Cruse Bereavement Care
    website: www.cruse.org.uk
    telephone: 0844 477 9400
    email: helpline@cruse.org.uk

Winston's Wish, the charity for bereaved children
    website: www.winstonswish.org.uk
    telephone: 08452 03 04 05
    email: info@winstonswish.org.uk

NHS Choices, for non-urgent medical advice
    telephone: 111

a note on the editors

Jonathan Bate is a well-known literary scholar. The author of many books on Shakespeare, his biographies of John Clare and Ted Hughes were both shortlisted for Britain's most prestigious non-fiction award, the Samuel Johnson Prize.

Paula Byrne is a bestselling author and Chief Executive of The Bibliotherapy Foundation. She has written biographies of, among others, Jane Austen and Evelyn Waugh.

Sophie Ratcliffe teaches English at Oxford University and is a Fellow and Tutor at Lady Margaret Hall. She fell in love with poetry when she read John Donne's 'A Valediction Forbidding Mourning' aged thirteen. Her desert island poems include 'Arrival' and 'To His Coy Mistress', and she'd take along a few songs by the Pet Shop Boys, too.

Andrew Schuman is a General Practitioner in the NHS, who also teaches doctors and medical students. He has always loved reading (and occasionally writing) poetry – often to escape the pressures of work. An insomniac, he does most of his reading between the hours of one and three a.m.

Mark Williams, who contributed the Afterword, is Emeritus Professor of Clinical Psychology and Honorary Senior Research Fellow in the Department of Psychiatry at the University of Oxford and was Director of the Oxford Mindfulness Centre until his retirement in 2013. Along with colleagues John Teasdale (Cambridge) and Zindel Segal (Toronto), he developed Mindfulness-based Cognitive Therapy for prevention of relapse and recurrence in major depression. He is the co-author, with Danny Penman, of the international bestseller *Mindfulness: A Practical Guide to Finding Peace in a Frantic World.*

permissions

index of poets